Sustainable Investing

Sustainable Investing

An ESG Starter Kit for Everyday Investors

Kylelane Purcell and Ben Vivari
Co-Founders of Till Investors

Foreword by
Jon Hale, Global Head of Sustainability Research
at Morningstar, Inc.

BEP
BUSINESS EXPERT PRESS
Leader in applied, concise business books

First published in 2023 by
Business Expert Press, LLC
222 East 46th Street, New York, NY 10017
www.businessexpertpress.com

ISBN-13: 978-1-63742-510-7 (paperback)
ISBN-13: 978-1-63742-511-4 (e-book)

Business Expert Press Environmental and Social Sustainability for Business Advantage Collection

First edition: 2023

10 9 8 7 6 5 4 3 2 1

Description

The Essential Starting Point for Values-Driven Investors

You are passionate about the important issues facing our world: Climate change. Racial justice. Gender equality. And you do things to reflect those passions—volunteering, donating, voting, and recycling. But there's an even more powerful way to advocate for what matters to you: Changing your investments.

Sustainable investing empowers individual investors to move their savings away from companies and funds that are harming the planet and into investments that are pushing for a cleaner, greener, and more just world. This isn't a niche strategy—there are hundreds of sustainable funds on the market and over a trillion dollars already invested in what are known as "ESG" funds—funds that consider the **E**nvironmental, **S**ocial, and **G**overnance aspects of the companies they invest in, as well as their financial performance.

Sustainable investing is more accessible, more actionable, and more achievable now than ever before, and this book is perfect for individuals looking to make their first sustainable investments. It contains useful and practical guidance on how to understand your choices in the rapidly expanding world of sustainable investing, and it offers concrete steps to invest in funds and companies that reflect your values.

Keywords

sustainable investing; ESG investing; socially responsible investing; ESG books; ESG investing CFA; how to invest sustainably; responsible investment; ethical investing; greenwashing

Contents

Testimonials ix

Foreword xi

Introduction xv

Chapter 1   Why Be a Sustainable Investor? 1

Chapter 2   What Is Sustainable Investing Today? 5

Chapter 3   What Makes a Company Sustainable? 11

Chapter 4   Will Sustainable Investing Cost Me Money? ...23

Chapter 5   The Ladder of Impact—or—What It Looks Like
             to Become a Sustainable Investor 35

Chapter 6   The Three Fighting Styles—The Key to Finding
             the Right Fund for You....................................45

Chapter 7   How to Be a Great Greenwashing Detective ...57

Chapter 8   Making the Move to Sustainable Funds 75

Chapter 9   Do I Need an Advisor to Invest Sustainably? ...85

Chapter 10   Amp Your Impact With Action......................91

Appendix: Fund Manager Profiles..99

About the Authors...119

Index 121

Testimonials

"This book helps each of us to look into the mirror and see an empowered person staring back—ready to use the influence of our wealth to co-create a livable world based on justice and sustainability."—**Andrew Behar, CEO of As You Sow**

"To invest sustainably does not have to be complicated nor should it be detrimental to financial performance: Kylelane Purcell and Ben Vivari provide a straightforward approach for investors with solid advice and acumen. I highly recommend for new investors who are strongly considering sustainable investing strategies."—**Jennifer Coombs, Director of Client Services, Ethos ESG**

"Ties directly in with people's understanding of finance and how it doesn't have to be separate from the kind of person you want to be. I really love the relatable examples—it's a great way to have the reader say, I want to do this and I can do this!"—**David Neun, Learning Experience Designer at State Employees Credit Union**

"I love the book—it's fun and interesting and doesn't read like a typical investment guide."—**Bonnie Maize, Sustainable Financial Advisor**

"I'd love to see your book help more investors realize that truly impactful investments are accessible to them as well."—**Laura Oldanie, Green Living and Money Coach and Founder of Rich and Resilient Living**

"I found it very readable and pitched at a good level for the investor who's just starting out."—**Casey Aspin, Editor at Principles for Responsible Investment (PRI)**

"The easiest parts to read are the examples of the companies. It helps people see why it makes a difference to choose the right investments."—**Kristin Rodriguez, Sustainable Financial Advisor**

Foreword

Whether we are recycling at home, deciding what kind of food to eat, purchasing consumer goods, deciding where we want to live and work, or choosing a profession, many of us consider sustainability in both our everyday choices and the bigger life decisions we make. We do so because we are concerned about things such as climate change and the environment, economic fairness, and whether our existing environmental, economic, and social systems literally can sustain life and prosperity on planet Earth for subsequent generations. Most of us want to make a difference in the world even if only in our own modest way, because that reflects who we are. It should come as no surprise that those of us who routinely apply a sustainability lens to the decisions that we make in the rest of our lives would want to do the same thing when it comes to our investments.

Doing so is not unlike what we do when we make consumer decisions. Just as an automobile is a product designed to meet our transportation needs, a mutual fund or exchange-traded fund (ETF) is an investment product designed to meet our financial goals. An electric vehicle (EV) meets our utilitarian need for transportation, but unlike cars with internal combustion engines, an EV does so with zero emissions, also benefiting people and planet, which makes it a better choice for the sustainably minded consumer. Similarly, a sustainable fund is one that meets our need for a risk-adjusted return on our investment while also leaving a positive impact on people and planet, making it a better choice for the sustainably minded investor.

Sustainable products, including investments, not only have a broader impact, but they provide us personally with what behavioral economists call expressive and emotional benefits in addition to their basic utilitarian benefits. Making a sustainable investment decision expresses who we are and makes us feel good about ourselves for making a decision that is aligned with our values. This, in turn, helps us become better investors, because we feel more closely connected to our investments. They are part of something bigger that's having a positive impact on the world. That connection helps us become better, more-disciplined investors, and more likely to stay the course during periods of market turmoil when many investors are abandoning ship. Sustainable investing can help us be more successful long-term investors because it aligns with our financial, social, and environmental goals.

All that said, it can be a challenge to figure out where to start on your sustainable investing journey. This book provides you with an excellent starting point. It will help you understand your own sustainability preferences. Perhaps you want to avoid making money from business activities that you don't believe are good for people and the planet. Or perhaps you simply want to make sure climate and other sustainability risks are fully accounted for in your investments. You may want your investments to have a positive impact on climate change, for example, or on how corporations are run to benefit workers and communities in addition to shareholders.

You will also find that you are not alone in your sustainable investing journey. This field of investing has experienced explosive growth over the past few years. For many fund managers, incorporation of environmental, social, and corporate governance (ESG) criteria to better assess investment risks and opportunities has become routine. Most of the world's largest public companies are addressing the ESG issues that affect their business, albeit to varying degrees. Many have begun to place sustainability at the forefront of their corporate strategy.

This book will help you understand the dizzying array of sustainable fund choices available today.

Sustainable investing is not a single narrowly constructed investment strategy that is practiced the same way by every fund manager. Think of sustainable investing as an umbrella term that contains a range of different approaches. A given sustainable fund may employ a single approach, such as exclusionary screening, or several approaches, such as combining exclusionary screening with selection of companies that are "best-in-class" on sustainability criteria relative to peers, and shareholder engagement with companies on sustainability issues they face. You will learn how to find the right sustainable fund for you, how to assess costs, and how to transition an existing portfolio to a sustainable one. If you are looking to make your first sustainable investment, this book will help you go forward with confidence as you do your part to become a better investor, while also making a difference in the world.

—Jon Hale
Global Head of Sustainability Research at Morningstar, Inc.
Spring 2023

Introduction

Congratulations on taking the first step toward becoming a sustainable investor! You're going to find this journey exciting, illuminating, sometimes frustrating, empowering, and at the end of the day, rewarding. How do we know?

Because we're sustainable investors ourselves.

Not so long ago, we were in your shoes—wanting to move our savings away from companies that were harming the world around us, and into funds that reflected our values.

But we were also approaching this problem from a unique vantage point. Because in our professional lives, we manage communications for some of the fund providers and financial advisors who are trying to sell the very funds we were looking to buy. We've spent decades managing the development of white papers, investment commentaries, and marketing materials for the investment industry.

As we went through the process of researching and choosing our first personal sustainable investments, speaking with asset managers and advisors, we learned a lot of great lessons about how to market their funds, how to describe what they do, and how to explain the importance of what they were doing.

But we learned a lot more about what it takes to be a sustainable investor. And those lessons form the basis for this book, and our sustainable investing initiative, Till Investors. Through the Till Investors website and in person, we are helping investors big and small—and their advisors—understand what sustainability means in the business world and the many potential benefits it offers. We're doing seminars, webinars, speeches, videos, and podcasts. We want to get the word out and clear up misconceptions.

This book is part of that effort, but we want to take it a step further. So, our goal for this book is to ***prepare you to invest in your first*** *sustainable fund.* To get there, we're going to cover some important topics about the sustainable investing industry, including:

- What "sustainable" means in the investment industry;
- The different ways a fund can promote sustainability; and
- How funds and companies greenwash—and how to avoid it.

We're also going to cover some important topics about you, the sustainable investor, including:

- Your place on the "ladder of impact" and how your sustainable options change as you advance along your investing journey;
- How a sustainable investment fits alongside the rest of your investment portfolio; and
- Where you can go to find sustainable investing options that fit your needs while not creating a lot of work for yourself.

Finally, we provide you with some profiles of some of the largest sustainable investing options out there today to boil down your options to something manageable.

But before we get started, a few things to know:

1. While we are approaching this as an introduction to sustainable investing, we are assuming that there are some basic concepts about investing in general that our readers are comfortable with. If you're not familiar with, say, the difference between an active and passive fund, or you're not sure what the S&P 500 is, that's ok. Don't be afraid to lean on online resources like Investopedia to help you out when you get to a concept you need a little help on.

2. In this book, we're going to talk about specific companies and funds. We're going to *name names*. But don't misunderstand—these are not recommendations to invest in this specific fund or those particular stocks. We are not licensed financial advisors, and we are not certified to sell anything. That also means we're not *trying* to sell you

anything. We have no association with any of the funds or fund managers mentioned in this book. What you are getting from us is completely independent, and focused on the *process* you use to invest sustainably—not the end result of what you invest in.

3. Finally, the world of sustainable investing is moving—fast. Every few months we see new regulations, new funds, and new initiatives. The best way to stay on top of these is to visit us at tillinvestors.com and sign up for our newsletter, or give us a follow on social media. Even better—tell us about your first sustainable investment and why you made it!

A Word on Stocks Versus Funds

As an individual investor, your two primary choices are investing in securities (stocks and bonds) or investing in funds (mutual funds, index funds, and exchange-traded funds).

In this guide, we want to focus on the basics and make sure they are understandable and usable for all investors. For that reason, our main focus is going to be on funds.

Why? Because funds are the most appropriate investment for the largest number of people. Funds pool money from many investors and invest the assets in a diversified portfolio of many stocks. Diversification is a proven way to limit your overall risk and expand the opportunity for making money. Funds require minimal effort, can be relatively inexpensive, and often don't require large upfront investments.

Being a sustainable investor is going to change the way you think about your money and your place in the world. And the best part is, the more people that invest sustainably, the more impact we are going to have at some of the largest companies in the world. Let's dive in.

CHAPTER 1

Why Be a Sustainable Investor?

You are passionate about the very important issues facing our world: Climate change. Racial justice. Gender equality. And you do things big and small to reflect those passions—buying green products, donating to causes you care about, voting, and recycling. But there's an even more powerful way to advocate for what matters to you: Changing your investments.

Investing is one of the most consequential things you can do with your money—it impacts your future, and the future of the businesses, products, and employees you invest in. Investing is sometimes talked about as if it is just a way to make money. But the picture is much broader than that. An investment in any company is both an endorsement of its approach and an opportunity to profit from its business practices. That is true whether you are investing directly in a stock, or indirectly through a mutual fund, index fund, or exchange-traded fund.

Historically, individual investors just didn't have access to good information about how a company went about making its money. That's not true any longer. There's a tremendous amount of focus being placed on company behaviors and the real-world impacts they have on their customers, employees, the environment, and their communities.

And as a result, aligning your investments with your personal values is now a thing you can do. In fact, it's surprising to imagine that you shouldn't do this. Where else in your life do you make decisions without your values in mind?

The Sustainability Instinct and the
Circle of Change

It's instinct to want to leave a positive mark on the world. We want to help earnest people succeed while holding those who do harm to account. We teach our children values, and we volunteer and donate to help our communities.

But you can't ignore the role that money plays in driving change. Substantive, lasting change almost always demands a strong financial base of support.

Money is like manure: it's only good if you spread it around.
—popular English expression

Investment is the financial system's way of determining what has value and encouraging good ideas to grow. When you make a purchase, you are adding to a company's balance sheet and giving its owners a small bit of profit. But when you invest, you make a much bolder statement. You are saying, I believe in you, and I want to put my money into your hands because I believe you can do good things that we can both benefit from.

Being a sustainable investor goes a step further. It puts pressure on company leadership to measure the human or environmental impacts of their decisions. It puts pressure on professional investors to ask tougher questions about the companies they invest in. Companies need investors, so the more investors ask those questions, the more motivated those companies are to improve their practices.

For example, a company can *say* that diversity hiring practices are important. But if that company knows that diversity hiring data will be included in investing decisions and that it will be measured against other companies on that basis? Well, that makes a big difference, and it turns the wheel of change.

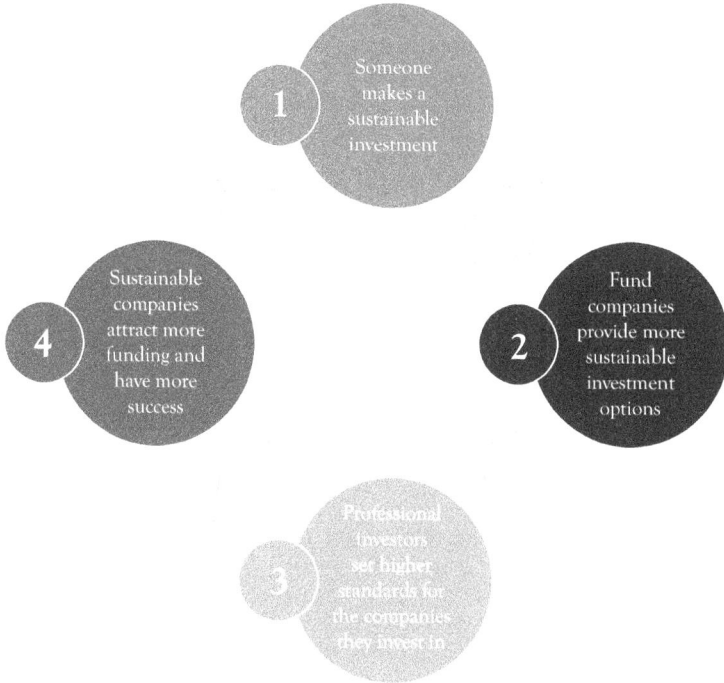

The diagram shows a cycle with four numbered circles:

1. Someone makes a sustainable investment
2. Fund companies provide more sustainable investment options
3. Professional investors set higher standards for the companies they invest in
4. Sustainable companies attract more funding and have more success

Sustainable Means Healthy, Today and in the Future

Being a sustainable investor makes an important statement. It tells your community, and the entire financial industry, that you don't accept destructive or deceptive ways to make money. It declares that you are part of the solution. But it also means that you are someone who is thoughtful about your own financial responsibilities and looking for ways to grow your money with companies that are thinking about the long term.

Broadly, sustainable investors care about both definitions of sustainability. Some care more about the "investor" aspect—they want to grow their financial resources steadily and consistently over time—while others started focusing on the social and environmental impacts of corporate decisions. Either way, sustainable investors have more reason to be satisfied by their choices, and more levers to pull to make real change in the world.

Investing has a (well-earned) reputation for being confusing and complicated. But here's a secret—when you start with your values in mind, your investment decisions will always seem easier to make, easier to understand, and easier to succeed with. Markets go up and down, but who you are and what you care about is fundamental.

In Short...

Different people have different values and priorities. But sustainable investors have something in common—they broadly stand for the principles of respect, responsibility, and productivity. They want to use their money to encourage those values, and they want to be aligned with businesses that do the same.

This desire isn't some kind of new-fangled, out-of-the-blue change to the investment landscape—it's been around for a long time. We'll get into more specifics about sustainability in Chapter 3, but before we do, let's take a brief look at the history of sustainable investing and where it stands today.

CHAPTER 2

What Is Sustainable Investing Today?

Here's something to chew on. Sustainable investing is exploding in popularity, and at the same time, it's almost unheard of by everyday people.

Let's look at some data to show you what we mean. According to the Forum for Sustainable and Responsible Investment, also known as US SIF, assets in sustainable investment funds were at $8.4 trillion by 2022. Yet of that figure, only $1.2 trillion was held in registered investment companies—the kind of publicly available mutual funds, exchange-traded funds, and other vehicles most commonly used by everyday investors. The remaining assets—more than three-quarters of the total—are primarily held in private investments only accessible to highly wealthy people and large institutions.

So, while the world of sustainable investments has grown rapidly, that growth has mostly come from big players. That's not to say, though, that the universe of public sustainable funds isn't growing. That $1.2 trillion figure has captured the attention of fund providers and led to a proliferation of sustainable fund options for the average investor.

Number of Sustainable Funds By Year

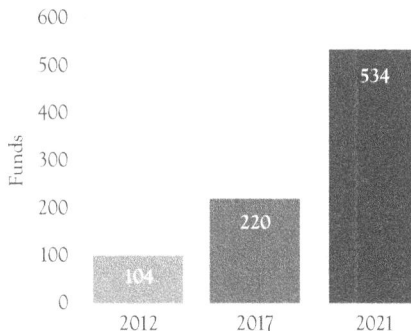

Morningstar Direct. Data as of December 31, 2021
www.morningstar.com/lp/sustainable-funds-landscape-report.

Even so, the average investor is still in the dark about it. A Gallup poll in 2021 found that 4 in 10 investors had never heard of sustainable investing, and only one in four had heard anything substantial about it.

U.S. Investors' Awareness of Sustainable Investing

How much have you heard or read about this type of investing, sometimes known as "sustainable investing," before now?

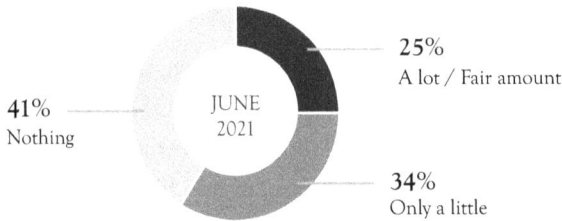

25%
A lot / Fair amount

41%
Nothing

JUNE
2021

34%
Only a little

Gallup Panel. Based on U.S. adults, aged 18 and older, with $10,000 or more invested in stocks, bonds, or mutual funds. Data as of June 2021.
https://news.gallup.com/poll/353879/investor-familiarity-sustainable-investing-remains-low.aspx.

So, if you're not familiar with the idea of investing sustainably, don't fret. You've got plenty of company. But the question is: why? How is it possible for sustainable investing to be so massive and yet so little known?

An answer can be found in the long and winding history of sustainable investing strategies, which started out as a kind of unloved niche within the financial industry.

The Origins of Sustainable Investing

The idea of investing with a set of values in mind is actually not very new at all. "Socially responsible" mutual funds have existed since the 1960s, using sustainable values like protecting the environment or treating workers fairly. Even earlier, faith-based investors sought to avoid "sin stocks"—that is, industries they find objectionable, such as alcohol and tobacco, pornography, and gambling.

These initial sustainable investments all had important limitations. It was easy to avoid companies if you didn't like their product or industry, but it was hard to peer into companies and evaluate how sustainable their business operations were. The data just wasn't available. Moreover, very few professional investors even bothered to ask those questions—the concept of a "sustainability analyst" didn't exist.

And yet, socially responsible funds persisted. Even though the "profit at any cost" type of investment analyst often scoffed at the idea, investors themselves often asked—even demanded—a chance to invest their values. So sustainable funds continued to occupy a small corner of the investment landscape for decades.

Early Sustainable Investors
From Investopedia, "A History of Impact Investing"

Socially responsible investing's origins in the United States began in the 18th century with Methodism, a denomination of Protestant Christianity that eschewed the slave trade, smuggling, and conspicuous consumption, and resisted investments in companies manufacturing liquor or tobacco products or promoting gambling. . . .

Socially responsible investing ramped up in the 1960s when Vietnam War protestors demanded that university endowment funds no longer invest in defense contractors. . . .

The combined efforts of protests and responsible investing during the Vietnam War and Apartheid in South Africa led to institutional and legislative change.

www.investopedia.com/news/history-impact-investing/

In the 21st century, things started to change—sustainable investing grew slowly but steadily. One seminal event was the establishment of the Principals of Responsible Investment by the United Nations in 2006, which encouraged investors to consider sustainability factors when investing. The BP oil spill in the Gulf of Mexico in 2010, which demonstrated how environmental factors could be directly linked to financial returns, also raised awareness. Rising concerns about climate change and the effect it has on businesses (and the effect that businesses have on climate change) also brought increased attention to sustainable investing. All of these laid important groundwork for the change to come.

And then, the heavy hitters came to play.

The Heavy Hitters Change the Game

In this case, the heavy hitters are "institutional" investors. These large organizations, which include pension funds, college endowments, foundations, and large nonprofits, typically manage millions or even billions of dollars. And most of them consider themselves to be "mission driven"— that is, they exist to serve the needs *and values* of their constituency.

As more and better reporting about company practices came to light, these organizations became concerned. What if their investments were actually working against the mission and values they stand for? Should a long-term retirement investor invest in a company that is contributing heavily to future climate disasters? Should an animal rights nonprofit invest in firms that test products on animals?

When institutional investors started asking these questions, the investment industry needed answers. And in the decade or so since, there has been a widespread response across the industry to develop and provide those answers. Sustainability ratings, impact assessments, industrywide working groups, and conferences—all of these have emerged as a response to demand from institutional investors.

In just the last few years, this exercise has started to produce additional options for what the industry calls "retail" investors—people like you.

The desire to invest your values goes back a long ways, but it has evolved as people have gotten better access to data and information about corporate behaviors and their impacts.

Pre-1960s	1960s–1990s	2000s	2010s to present
Faith-based strategies	Socially responsible investing (SRI)	Corporate social responsibility	Environmental, Social and Governance (ESG)
Avoidance of "Sin Stocks"	Early efforts to define and measure socially responsible companies	Enhanced access to data and news about corporate behaviors	Dramatic growth in data about ESG attributes and impact

In Short...

The combination of rising demand, new strategies, and better data has disrupted the entire investment industry. Very quickly, sustainable investing funds have grown dramatically in number and type over the past decade. Sustainable investing is becoming:

- **More Accessible.** There are now hundreds of mutual funds, index funds, and exchange-traded funds (ETFs) that use some form of sustainability strategy.
- **More Actionable.** Sustainable investment funds are now showing up more often in company retirement plans (such as 401ks, 403bs, and various workplace IRAs) and college saving plans (such as 529s). They're not available in every plan, but they are becoming more common, giving you more avenues to pursue sustainable investing.
- **More Achievable.** Sustainable investors are impacting companies in ways that were unheard of even five years ago, using company engagement and proxy votes to demand improvements in company leadership and operational policies.

Today, it is more realistic for you to invest according to your values than ever before. But taking advantage of this opportunity requires some thought—some self-reflection even. Why? Because there is no one definition of "sustainable" and no standardized way to measure it. The key to success in sustainable investing is understanding what *you* mean by sustainable, and then finding options that match your viewpoint.

That may sound complicated, but we think we can boil it down with a few examples.

CHAPTER 3

What Makes a Company Sustainable?

When you become a sustainable investor, you put your money into sustainable strategies that are trying to identify sustainable companies. But "sustainable" can mean a lot of things to a lot of different people. So before looking at sustainable investing strategies or funds, let's first discuss what a sustainable company generally looks and acts like.

Or at least, what the investment industry thinks about it.

It's important to say at the outset that true sustainability can be hard for most companies to achieve. Companies don't have perfect information, and they must deal with competition and risk and cash flow challenges and taxes and laws and ... well, the list runs on. Companies must prioritize their own survival, sometimes at the cost of the interests of others. But importantly, this reality doesn't mean that companies must, or should, throw away the goals of sustainability altogether. Broadly speaking, quality sustainable companies are the ones that consistently endeavor to be more sustainable. When we use the phrase "sustainable companies" in this book, this is what we are talking about.

What does this look like in practice? Having talked with many different investors, fund managers, companies, and associations, we've found that the broadest way to define a sustainable company looks something like this:

A "sustainable" company is one that generates long-term profits while peacefully coexisting with the people and planet around it.

The financial industry has tried to capture this sentiment in many catchphrases and terms over the years.

- In the early 2000s, investors tried to define what "corporate social responsibility" looked like and which companies were trying to manage themselves in this way.

- Another popular term over the past 20 years has been "triple bottom line," where companies balance the needs of people, planet, and profit.
- More recently, the phrase "stakeholder capitalism" has become common—the belief that companies need to balance the interests of profit-minded shareholders with the concerns of employees, customers, and communities.
- Today the buzzword is ESG, which stands for "Environmental, Social, and Governance," and refers to various ways of analyzing and engaging with companies based on quantifiable data in these three areas.

All of these phrases are just different takes on how to define a company that can last for a long time. That's why we prefer the term sustainable. Sustainability is an excellent shorthand for the qualities that make a company successful in the long term—smart financial decisions, inclusive employee practices, good management of natural resources, quality customer service, and so on. It's a reasonable expectation for customers and investors alike.

Sustainability is an excellent shorthand for the qualities that make a company successful in the long term.

So if you invest in a sustainable mutual fund—that is, a fund that invests in a lot of sustainable companies—it is reasonable to expect that all the companies represented in that fund will meet that broad definition of "sustainable." But there is a *lot* of room for interpretation and opinion within these broad guidelines. There are many judgment calls to be made along the way.

In this chapter, we're going to dig into what some of those judgment calls look like. This will help you understand the thought processes that professional investors use to identify sustainable companies. Perhaps more importantly, it will help you think about what *you* consider to be a sustainable company. In the end, funds that look different represent an opportunity for you to find one that most closely matches your own definition of sustainability.

What Are We Aiming for?

If we can agree that sustainability takes a long-term view, what does that view look like? If the concern is people and the planet alongside profit, what is it about those people and this planet that are we hoping for?

It's a huge question, and well-meaning people can get bogged down in debates regarding different visions of sustainability. Fortunately, though, there is an answer referenced pretty widely in sustainability circles.

This comprehensive definition of sustainability was developed by the United Nations, and it is called the Sustainable Development Goals (SDGs). To create the SDGs, the United Nations talked with investors, financial experts, governments, nonprofits, policy makers … virtually any group that tries to identify and address global economic and social concerns. They then organized that input into 17 high-level goals to achieve a more economically robust, environmentally sustainable, and socially just world. The goals were established in 2015 with an aim of accomplishing them by 2030.

To be clear, the SDGs were primarily designed to be policy goals—that is, to help guide governments and political movements. Nonetheless, a great many investment funds use the SDGs to explain how their strategies line up with a broader vision of a sustainable future.

As a sustainable investor, you will run into the SDGs often, and we find them to be a useful way to think through the kinds of issues a fund prioritizes in evaluating sustainable companies. It's also the place where sustainable funds start to diverge from one another. One might focus more on climate action. Another might pay more attention to addressing poverty or hunger. Some care a lot about social impact, while others prioritize more traditional financial analysis.

They serve another valuable purpose too because they can help you consider which aspects of sustainability are most important to you. Defining your own vision of sustainability is an incredibly helpful step in figuring out which companies meet your sustainability standards. There is no right or wrong answer, but your answer can help lead you to strategies that are in-line with your personal priorities.

Regardless of which goals a fund is most concerned with, certain goals are going to be more relevant for some companies than others. That's where the next level of analysis comes in: Materiality.

These are all of the United Nations' Sustainable Development Goals. There's no shortage of items on the world's to-do list!

Which Sustainable Matters? Materiality

Whether you are looking at sustainability through the lens of the SDGs or some other scheme, certain issues are going to matter more to some companies than others. A U.S.-based clothing store needs a different kind of sustainability strategy than a global coffee bean supplier. This is where "materiality" comes into play—meaning, the relevance of certain sustainability factors to a particular company or industry.

Materiality is one of those common-sense concepts that gets tricky when you dive into the details. Obviously, for example, a major accounting firm doesn't need to have a policy about manufacturing pollutants—it's just not that material to their business. On the other hand, they might need a much more robust corporate code of ethics than, say, a factory, because even a small slippage in their standards could lead to mass financial fraud. But again, even well-meaning people can disagree on what is material to whom, so there need to be standards.

Like with the SDGs, there is a widely available, built-by-consensus tool for determining materiality, and this one is run by the Sustainability Accounting Standards Board (SASB), a nonprofit organization established in 2011. SASB's Materiality Map lines up a list of industries and plots them against a list of sustainability issues, creating a roadmap for determining which sustainability issues are most relevant for each industry.

For example, according to SASB, for large retailers like Target or Walmart, issues like employee engagement and labor practices are particularly important, while issues like wastewater management aren't as big of a concern. Conversely, for a large food producer like Conagra, wastewater management is a very important issue, while employee engagement is less important than managing an ethical supply chain.

As a sustainable investor, you will run into discussions about materiality a lot. And every fund will have its own spin on it. While some funds will talk about it more explicitly than others, almost all funds use it to narrow down the specifics of what to look for with a particular type of company. It is another judgment call that drives differences among sustainable funds.

One Small Slice of a Materiality Map

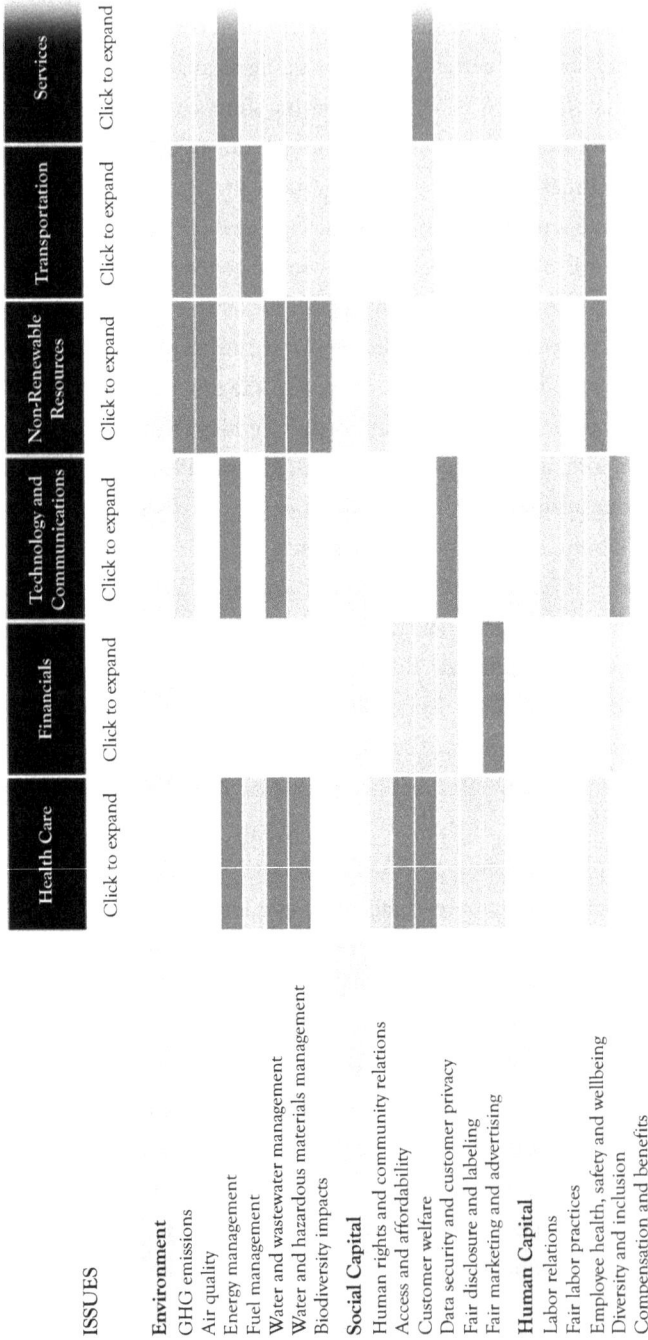

ISSUES	Health Care	Financials	Technology and Communications	Non-Renewable Resources	Transportation	Services
	Click to expand	Click to expand	Click to expand	Click to expand	Click to expand	Click to expand
Environment						
GHG emissions						
Air quality						
Energy management						
Fuel management						
Water and wastewater management						
Water and hazardous materials management						
Biodiversity impacts						
Social Capital						
Human rights and community relations						
Access and affordability						
Customer welfare						
Data security and customer privacy						
Fair disclosure and labeling						
Fair marketing and advertising						
Human Capital						
Labor relations						
Fair labor practices						
Employee health, safety and wellbeing						
Diversity and inclusion						
Compensation and benefits						

This is what a materiality map looks like—a tool that professional money managers use to identify which sustainability issues they should consider as they invest funds on behalf of their shareholders

Source: SASB www.sasb.org/standards/materiality-map/.

Filling Out the Scorecard

A professional investment analyst who is assessing a company for sustainability now has two important pieces of the puzzle in place. The SDGs help define the overall goals, and SASB's map helps establish which companies have an impact on attaining those goals (or not). The next step is to identify the company decisions and practices that create those impacts and then to evaluate the company's performance on those factors.

This is both an art and a science, working with the best data available and supporting that with qualitative research. Let's take a look at what that might look like.

Consider a fund analyst who is trying to assess a company's performance related to carbon emissions. Unfortunately, there is no enforced global standardized reporting system for carbon emissions. But the analyst can use other information to help their decision. Has the company made a Net Zero pledge, in-line with an emissions-reducing program run by the United Nations? Has the company joined other industry efforts to address climate change? Larger fund companies are often able to meet independently with company executives to ask pressing questions about this issue and others. All these inputs can go into a judgment on the company's climate efforts.

As another example, imagine a fund that is focused on racial diversity. Like with carbon emissions, there is no standardized global reporting requirement for things like the racial makeup of a company's workforce or equality of pay across employees of different races. But the manager could look at the diversity of a company's board of directors or executive team. The manager could also look more favorably upon companies that *do* disclose data on the race and compensation of their employees.

Sometimes, funds use a team of analysts to evaluate each company individually. In other cases, they might create an index of sustainable companies based on a set of standard quantitative guidelines. In still other cases, they might partner with an outside firm that already has a method of evaluating corporate sustainability and just use their findings. None of these strategies are necessarily "right" or "wrong"—they are simply different ways to get to an outcome.

We wouldn't suggest that everyday investors try to evaluate exactly how their funds are scoring companies on these measures—in truth, funds rarely provide meaningful detail on what their scorecards look like anyway. There's a simpler way for you to sift through the different approaches funds use, which we'll discuss more in coming chapters.

At this stage, it's useful to understand that there is no single definition of a sustainable company, and there can be lots of honest disagreements. For us, it's one more bit of evidence that the key to sustainable investing is finding which strategies are the best fit for what you care about.

The Tesla Example

Let's take a look at how some funds arrive at their conclusions by examining a controversial company in the sustainable investing world today: Tesla.

Every company has things that it does well and things that it could improve on. Areas where they act in the best interests of the people and planet around them and areas where they could go further. In Tesla's case, those plusses and negatives are sometimes extreme.

On the good side is the product itself. Tesla's electric vehicles are much more sustainable than the gas-powered alternatives on the market. Tesla's technology innovations helped demonstrate that EVs could be profitable and showed that the changeover from gas stations to charging stations was doable. Without Tesla's leadership, the current EV revolution may not have happened.

If that was all we knew about Tesla, they would be an easy addition to any sustainable fund or portfolio. But there is a lot more to the story.

- Tesla has had significant challenges with lawsuits related to racial discrimination toward their employees.
- While their product is green, their manufacturing processes have run afoul of numerous environmental regulations in the United States and around the world.
- Their planned business line in autonomous cars has led to serious safety concerns both for Tesla drivers and passengers and the people around them.
- Their CEO, Elon Musk, has many outside interests and very little accountability to his board of directors.

Given what you know about Tesla, do they fit your vision of a sustainable company? Bear this in mind as we run through how the financial industry might evaluate the company.

What Some ESG Rating Agencies Say About Tesla

Tesla's many controversies make it a great example of how sustainability rating agencies go through the process of identifying sustainable companies. These rating agencies grade companies based on their sustainability profiles, and many fund managers use these grades to help them build portfolios of sustainable companies. Let's see what they have to say.

The first rating agency is MSCI—a global research, data, and technology provider to the financial industry. MSCI's sustainability ratings are well regarded and broadly used, as they try to capture a company's ability to jump on sustainability opportunities as well as avoid major risks.

MSCI reports the following regarding Tesla's performance on key material sustainability factors:

Tesla's ESG Profile—According to MSCI (December 2022)

ESG LAGGARD	AVERAGE	ESG LEADER
Product safety and quality	Corporate governance Labor management	Corporate behavior Product carbon footprint Opportunities in clean tech

In this table, MSCI shows what they consider to be material issues for Tesla. These issues line up well with what we discussed earlier—product safety is a big issue, corporate governance and labor management practices aren't great, but in terms of carbon footprint and clean technology of their final product, Tesla shines.

Taking all of these into account, MSCI comes up with the following ESG rating for Tesla.

Tesla's ESG Rating from MSCI (December 2022)

CCC	B	BB	BBB		AA	AAA

Tesla is   among 42 companies
in the automobiles industry.

Now, let's look at Sustainalytics, which is the sustainability rating wing of Morningstar. Sustainalytics is also a well-respected firm, but they are a little different from MSCI in that their primary focus is on identifying risks to the business that may stem from sustainability failures.

Sustainalytics identifies four "Top Material ESG Issues" for Tesla as of December 2022:

- Corporate governance
- Product governance
- Human capital
- Business ethics

They find that there have been ESG "controversies" regarding both corporate governance and labor relations. Generally speaking, controversies refer to business decisions that have been roundly criticized in the media, or other public forums, for creating some kind of harm (to employees, consumers, or others).

Tesla's ESG Rating from Sustainalytics (December 2022)

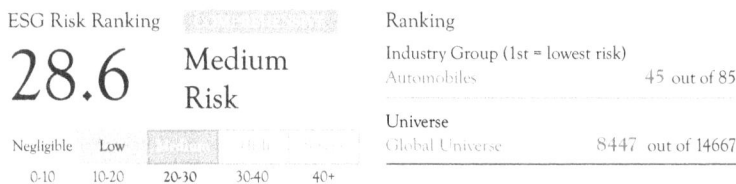

ESG Risk Ranking		Ranking	
28.6 Medium Risk		Industry Group (1st = lowest risk)	
		Automobiles	45 out of 85
		Universe	
Negligible Low		Global Universe	8447 out of 14667
0-10 10-20 20-30 30-40 40+			

In the end, Sustainalytics agrees with MSCI that Tesla is about average within its industry, although it puts more focus on highlighting the long-term risk the company may present.

What can we learn from looking at these two reports?

The first lesson to draw is that there is more to Tesla than its electric cars. Understanding a company's true sustainability characteristics demands a deeper look at its operations, its decision makers, and all the company's stakeholders. The good news is that quality sustainable strategies are doing this detailed work, and they are relying on services that are competing to provide better and better insight into sustainability issues.

On the other hand, there is a lot of variability in sustainability ratings, which is an indication that there are a lot of different views about how to characterize a sustainable company. Just looking at MSCI and Sustainalytics, for example:

- MSCI and Sustainalytics have very different starting points—Sustainalytics has a clear risk focus, while MSCI looks through a lens of both risk and opportunity.
- They also appear to be using different scoring strategies, as MSCI finds Tesla to be "Average" in corporate governance and labor management, while Sustainalytics finds that these are two of the biggest problem areas for the company.
- Finally, their grading approaches are completely different, with MSCI giving out broad letter grades, while Sustainalytics determines a number grade down to the 10th of a point.

All this variability makes it distractingly easy to poke holes in the effort to define sustainability. It makes it possible for greenwashers to cherry-pick good numbers while dismissing bad grades. It allows critics to highlight inconsistencies while obscuring harmful practices. Sometimes, it can give a company's competitors a stick to beat them with.

Of course, it's often the targets of criticism that are most likely to take this approach. Unsurprisingly maybe, Tesla's CEO Elon Musk became publicly and furiously angry when S&P, another large rating agency, removed Tesla from their ESG Index in 2022. But their reasoning was sound. S&P removed Tesla due to weak codes of conduct, discrimination, poor working conditions, and the questionable handling of an investigation into deaths and injuries involving their autonomous cars.

When the S&P balanced those negatives against the positives of electric cars, the balance fell to the negative. It's that simple. And comparing that decision with the ratings of MSCI and Sustainalytics, which found that Tesla was overall a net neutral in ESG, it doesn't seem far from conventional wisdom at all.

In Short …

If there's one takeaway from this chapter, it's this: there are different ideas about what makes for a sustainable company. There are also different approaches to defining and evaluating ESG factors in an investment strategy. And that's ok. In fact, it can be a good thing for the sustainable investor.

Sustainability is *subjective*. Every person, and every fund, has their own opinions about what matters most, what's really good, what's window dressing, and what's objectionable. Each rating agency and fund manager has a different setup for analyzing and presenting their opinions of a company.

This means that you have the *opportunity* to compare different funds and find one with a vision of sustainability that speaks to you. It means that you have *real choice* as to how your money is invested sustainably. We'll talk a lot more about how to do that later in this book.

By this point, you may be thinking that sustainable investing is interesting and something you think you could reasonably do. You might even be envisioning making your first sustainable investment! It's been our experience that once a person starts to think realistically about becoming a sustainable investor, one important question rises up for almost everyone:

Will sustainable investing cost me money?

CHAPTER 4

Will Sustainable Investing Cost Me Money?

This is the first question a lot of folks ask about sustainable investing, and it's an important one. The primary purpose of investing is to put yourself in a better financial position. That's better for you and your family, of course, but it also gives you more opportunity to make additional sustainable investments in the future. If investing sustainably is going to perform poorly, maybe it's not such a good idea.

Allow us to skip to the end and give you the answer: Investment performance does not need to be an impediment to the sustainable investor. In fact, if you're investing for the long term, sustainable strategies offer some significant advantages in terms of the potential returns you can get on your investment.

It's important to emphasize this message because there is a commonly held belief that "investing for good" means "not making any money." It's really great news to discover that's not typically the case. But let's discuss performance, risk, and cost in more detail. Having a clear set of expectations about what you can expect as a sustainable investor is very, very important.

First, the Big Picture

"Will sustainable investing cost me money" is a question that has been the subject of a lot of debate. Many financial experts have argued that sustainable companies have a fundamental flaw—they can't *possibly* be as successful as more traditional types of companies. They are "too distracted" by social concerns, they throw too much money at unproductive ideas, and their products are ultimately too expensive to be competitive.

This story has been kicking around for decades, and lots of people believe in it. If you have a financial advisor, you might well have heard some version of it. But you might be surprised to learn that this argument isn't based on any actual research or comparisons. It is largely an anecdotal belief.

And it turns out, the anecdote is wrong. Studies show that the returns for the average sustainable investment strategy are as good as, or better than, comparable traditional strategies.

We're not talking about a few studies, here or there. In the last 10 years, there has been an explosion in research dedicated to evaluating sustainability, both from a corporate and an investor point of view. Their conclusions can best be summed up by an NYU Stern Center meta-analysis from 2020. It reviewed more than 1,000 studies of sustainability performance and concluded that there is no predictable penalty, either for companies or investors, in focusing on sustainability.

Correlation between ESG and Financial Performance

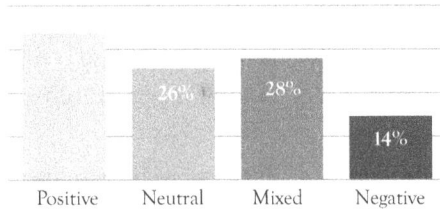

According to the NYU Stern mega study, sustainable investing strategies have mostly positive or neutral results, compared with traditional funds
www.stern.nyu.edu/sites/default/files/assets/documents/NYU-RAM_ESG-Paper_2021 Rev_0.pdf.

That's great news if you are the average sustainable investing strategy! But what does this "average opportunity for success" mean to you? Is sustainable investing going to cost *you* money?

Now the Real Deal

We at Till Investors are believers in sustainable investing, and we wouldn't be if we thought it would hurt you financially (or us for that matter). But we're just not comfortable leaving the conversation at "sustainable performs as well or better." There are some caveats we have to share.

First, not all sustainable funds, companies, or strategies are alike, so painting them all with the broad brush of "on average" can be misleading.

For example, many sustainable funds shy away from oil and gas companies, but there are exceptions to the rule. Some sustainable strategies are more concentrated and riskier than others. And anyway, you're not investing in "the average" fund. You're choosing a fund that may turn out to be above or below average.

Furthermore, sustainable strategies are constantly evolving, and so is the data those strategies use. Past success doesn't necessarily mean future success, especially as things change.

The most important point to remember is that sustainable investing is still investing. It has risk just like any other investment, and there are no guarantees. Sustainable companies can fail. Sustainable funds can underperform. And the reality is, sometimes sustainable funds do underperform the broader market, especially over narrow time periods.

Here's an example. In the first half of 2022, oil prices soared in the wake of the Russia/Ukraine war, and oil company stocks soared along with them. Sustainable strategies that avoid fossil fuels were left way behind, in comparison to the overall market. Circumstances like that are not all that unusual.

How does that jibe with studies saying that sustainability strategies perform the same or better than conventional funds? It's a short-term/long-term thing.

What Makes Sustainability Valuable?

In the short-term, sustainable investments are subject to market swings like any other investments. Look at any relatively short block of time and you're just as likely to see underperformance, compared to some generic market benchmark, as outperformance. That's true for every strategy under the sun. We've often noticed that during these stretches, the detractors come out like boobirds, citing underperformance as evidence of the supposed flaws of sustainable investing.

What was encouraging about the NYU Stern study is that it suggested that sustainable strategies are no more prone to these kinds of short-term market swings than more traditional funds are. And the report made this interesting observation:

"Improved financial performance due to ESG [that is, measures of sustainability] becomes more marked over longer time horizons."

Now that's a finding that really caught our eye. Almost every single investor is investing over longer time horizons—a new house in five years, a college education in 15 years, a retirement in 40 years. If there is a financial advantage to be gained by investing sustainably over these time periods, investors really need to know it.

There is a theory emerging that does a good job of explaining how and why sustainable investing can perform better over longer time horizons. This theory looks at sustainable investing as a form of *risk management.* Companies that are sustainable do a better job of acknowledging and addressing risk, leading to better long-run performance, even if it sometimes means sacrificing short-term gains.

For example:

- A company that acknowledges the risks to its business being brought by climate change may end up spending some additional money to address those risks in the short-term, but in the long term will be better positioned to face changing consumer preferences, evolving regulations, and, of course, a changed climate.
- A company that pays its employees well may have a higher line item for wages on its balance sheet. But it will also have a healthier and more committed workforce. It will avoid scrutiny from community leaders and regulators. And it doesn't have to worry about efforts to raise the minimum wage. Those things all pay off in the long run.

This theory plays out well looking at the empirical evidence. For example, the NYU Stern study found that sustainable strategies provide "downside protection"—that is, they tend to hold their value better during market slumps. This trend was on display in 2020: as COVID shut down the world, companies with better sustainability profiles held up better than the average company. A global pandemic is certainly a risk; sustainable companies appeared to be better prepared to face this risk. They were better prepared to "sustain," regardless of what happens in the economy.

Managing risk across all a company's stakeholders—their customers, employees, shareholders, regulators, and communities—is vital for a company's long-term success. How does this play out for sustainable investors? Let's start by looking at what can happen to a company that *doesn't* consider the risk across all its stakeholders.

Case Study #1: For-Profit Colleges

In the mid-to-late 2000s, for-profit colleges were all the rage in the investing world. They were generating huge revenues and massive returns for their investors. But only a few years later, the bubble burst. As an example, Corinthian Colleges had revenues of $1.7 billion in 2010—and by 2016 was completely out of business. Why?

Because their business model was *unsustainable*.

Like many other firms in its industry, Corinthian's approach wasn't creating value for their customers. They asked low-income students to borrow heavily, using government loans, ultimately saddling those students with huge debts and little hope of paying them off. Their promised value—that the students with degrees would turn into high-earning workers—simply wasn't coming true. And that represented a huge risk for the industry even as they were pulling in record revenues year after year.

In the short run, for-profit colleges were a viable investment. Potential students were looking for more accessible college options, and existing students wouldn't realize that their degrees had limited value until years later. But in the long run, the industry's primary customers were walking away dissatisfied. Anyone applying a sustainability lens to this industry would have seen huge red flags. And if you're investing for the long-term, betting against an unsustainable business model is a smart move.

Case Study #2: Juul e-Cigarettes

In the late 2010s, e-cigarettes were booming. No e-cigarette manufacturer was booming louder than Juul Labs. From a purely financial perspective, they were a fantastic investment. Only a few years old, they were earning nearly a billion dollars a year, and dominating market share against their competitors, with a valuation approaching $15 billion.

From a long-term sustainability perspective, though, Juul was a troubling investment. Juul existed for short-term profit but did a terrible job of looking forward and managing risk, preferring instead to rely on dishonest marketing to quiet concerns. It made claims that their product helped people quit smoking, but there was no evidence to back that up. They claimed that they were not marketing to teens but were selling e-cigarettes with flavors like "mango" and "crème brulee" which proved very popular among teens. Juul was operating in a very new marketplace that benefited from light regulation. But cigarettes overall face significant regulatory scrutiny, and there was a lot of uncertainty about how regulations might change.

For a long-term-minded sustainability investor, these factors were potential signs of trouble. But for the type of investor that focuses only on profit, Juul was irresistible. In 2018, cigarette manufacturer Altria stepped in and acquired a significant portion of Juul in a $13 billion deal. Red flags and all, Altria decided to place a large bet on the future success of Juul.

Fast forward to 2022. Just four years after the Altria purchase, Juul's chickens came home to roost. Regulators ramped up their focus on the way e-cigarettes were encouraging youth smoking, and the FDA announced plans to ban Juul products altogether. Altria took a *ninety-five percent hit* on their investment in Juul.

Like with for-profit colleges, there was a lot of short-term money to be made in e-cigarettes. But a long-term, sustainable investor would have seen the red flags, acknowledged the net negative, and rightly avoided the industry as a whole.

Sustainability as a Foundation for Long-Term Success

The previous two case studies lay out clear examples where an eye on long-term sustainability helped investors avoid poor businesses. What does it look like when sustainable decision making improves a company's outlook?

Positive sustainability stories are often less dramatic than negative ones, because sustainability is more about long-term viability than it is about short-term stock drama. But there are many examples of how ethical, sustainable thinking helped put companies in a stronger, more competitive position. Here are a couple of examples.

Case Study #3: Toyota

It's hard to imagine now, but Toyota Motor Corp was seen as taking a huge risk in 1997 when it first released the Prius hybrid. The dangers of climate change and CO_2 emissions were already well known in the scientific community, but the general response from the auto industry was to minimize or outright ignore the problem. In fact, as late as 2008, General Motors Vice Chairman Bob Lutz told reporters that he viewed global warming as a "total crock of shit."

But Toyota was an atypical company. In an industry that often focused on the latest cool designs and sold cars with nebulous ideas like "freedom" and "power," Toyota had a more practical mindset and an eye for the long term. The technology existed to make cars more efficient without making them more expensive. Hybrid engines would require less gas, and so would be cheaper for their owners. And if climate concerns kept growing—and there was every reason to think they might—hybrids would be far less likely to be affected by new regulation or legislation. That is to say, they would have *less risk*.

Fast forward 25 years, and it's clear that Toyota was right. The Prius and other Toyota hybrids have been global best-sellers. Toyota is today the largest-selling car company and one of the most profitable. Its stock results have been many multiples of what companies like, say, GM have provided their investors.

Today, Toyota finds itself facing a similar kind of critical moment. The company has been recently criticized for lobbying against electric vehicles (EVs), because it prefers a different technology—hydrogen fuel cells. To date, its hydrogen-based model has not proven popular, while EVs have become all the rage. Will Toyota once again be proven right?

It's hard to say with confidence, but that's part of the point. Companies have to make these kinds of strategic decisions all the time, and the implications of those decisions can affect company value for decades. At least Toyota has a track record—a very successful track record—at knowing how to identify and prioritize long-term value. So even if they are wrong today, you can have some confidence, as a long-term investor, that they will survive and thrive as a company.

Case Study #4: Intel

Intel is a semiconductor manufacturer, and one thing semiconductor manufacturers need is water. Lots and lots of water.

Clean water is essential to the process of creating and cleaning chips and in very—very—high volume. To the tune of billions of gallons each year. Intel may be a global company, but it can't produce its chips if water resources local to their factories are strained. That's a big risk for Intel (and its competitors too).

One of the biggest impacts of climate change has been dramatic challenges to local water management. Droughts and floods are increasingly common, and both greatly stress municipal water systems and the companies that rely on them. It's a challenge for companies like Intel today, and every report, study, and planning program says that it's a challenge that will only get worse.

But Intel isn't avoiding the problem, they're embracing it. Intel has become a global leader in developing water treatment systems that are highly efficient. This is risk management in action. The company works with local governments to build water recycling facilities to recover the water it uses. They were the first global tech company to establish water restoration goals in 2017, offsetting their freshwater use by contributing to water restoration projects. As of mid-2022, the firm announced that they restore more freshwater than they use in the United States, Costa Rica, and India.

How Will Intel Benefit?

Intel's commitment to water renewal comes, in part, from its manufacturing history in Arizona, which goes back to 1980. Arizona is an attractive location to build semiconductors—it has an educated workforce, low taxes, virtually no seismic activity (apparently this is important to semiconductor manufacturers), and ample opportunity to use solar power. But as a desert location, water can be hard to come by.

And that makes semiconductors a controversial industry for the state to support. The more water semiconductor makers use, the less might be available for the community or local farmers. Especially given the contentious history of water battles in the southwest, expanding in Arizona seemed like a risky play.

By making pledges about water restoration, and backing them up with major investments, Intel has demonstrated to Arizona that it is serious about sustainable water management. It has built strong relationships with municipal authorities and balanced the needs of community and customer stakeholders. And it has secured access to a critical resource for the long term while reducing the conflicts and risks that come with its use.

It has also shown the business world, and its competitors, the value of a more sustainable approach. In 2022, Taiwan Semiconductors Manufacturing also opened a plant in the Phoenix area, and like Intel, it made pledges around water restoration and invested in water treatment capabilities. This example shows how Intel's leadership helped make the entire industry more sustainable but also highlights how Intel remains way out in front of its competitors. Intel is betting that water restoration will be the key to its long-term survival and its ability to deliver value to shareholders in the future.

But Do Sustainable Funds Cost More to Invest In?

The data shows that sustainable companies are viable investments, at least in terms of their potential to grow your money over time. What about the cost to invest in them? Are sustainable funds pricey?

This is a fundamental issue, but it bears repeating: the performance of your investments will be impacted by the fees and expenses of the funds you invest in. Sales charges, trading fees, and annual expenses directly reduce the returns you receive as an investor. That's true for every investment. Is there anything unique about the costs of sustainable funds?

Yes...in a way.

As a group, sustainable funds are not the cheapest funds you can find. A 2020 study from Morningstar found that there is a premium, or "greenium," being charged by sustainable funds, on average. While the asset-weighted average expense ratio on sustainable funds clocked in at 0.61 percent, the same average for traditional funds was 0.41 percent. That's a meaningful difference.

But it's not the whole story. The same study highlighted the role that active versus passive strategies play in the overall averages. Passive strategies are designed to track an index. They don't do research or make their own investment choices, and their trading approaches are more or less automated. That makes them very cheap to run. There are a lot of index funds in the traditional fund space, and those funds are hugely popular.

Index funds are somewhat less common in the sustainable space. That's not to say that there are no valid passive sustainable funds—there are several. But sustainability analysis isn't as standardized as traditional financial analysis is. Index funds can set some basic sustainability screens, but active strategies hire staff to evaluate individual companies and review a constantly evolving stream of environmental-, social-, and governance-related data. That effort costs money.

The Morningstar study showed that, if you exclude low-cost index funds from the spectrum of traditional mutual funds, and just focus on actively managed funds, the average asset-weighted expense ratio rises to 0.62 percent. That's about on par with the cost of the average sustainability fund.

Let's be clear. On average, you will be paying as much in expenses for sustainable strategies as you would for an actively managed mutual fund. So, when you make an investment in a sustainable strategy, you are saying, "I am willing to pay a bit more per year to make sure that sustainable criteria are being appropriately, and consistently, applied to my investments."

To us, that seems like a reasonable thing to pay for...up to a point.

If the expenses are higher than that 0.61 percent average, look a little closer. Sometimes those fees are legit—they may help an active manager do a better job of company research. But if that's the case, the fund should be able to state that clearly. If the fund can't explain what those expenses are paying for, it could be just a price tag with very little substance behind it.

Sustainable funds are priced like active traditional funds

	TRADITIONAL INDEX FUND	TRADITIONAL ACTIVELY MANAGED FUNDS	SUSTAINABLE FUNDS
Average asset weighted expense ratio	0.12%	0.61%	0.62%

Source: Morningstar.

In Short...

The case for sustainable investing is straightforward:

Sustainable companies set themselves up for success by identifying and creating things that have lasting value. Maybe it's a product, a technology, or a strategy; maybe it's a focus on relationship building and a knack for getting stakeholders to work together. Often, it's an understanding of what risks lie around the corner—risks their competitors can't or won't see.

Companies that prioritize things with lasting value win lasting fans. "Car people" were merciless when the Prius first came out, making fun of its bland design and modest engine strength. But buyers saw something different—a simple, inexpensive car that was reliable and cheap to fuel. And, it made a meaningful dent in the CO_2 emissions that were driving the climate crisis to boot. These features gave owners lasting value, and as a result, Priuses became more than a car—they became a cultural icon.

The data that we see on sustainable performance bears this case out. Companies that are prepared for the long run, and that are acknowledging and addressing big-picture risks, are building themselves up from a more solid base. It's not surprising to see these companies outperform in the long term, falter less in bad markets, and recover quicker when the market improves.

If you're a long-term investor—and virtually everyone is—this feels like the sweet spot. In the best-case scenario, your personal financial circumstances become more sustainable when you tie your investments to sustainable companies. It's a meaningful bonus that your improving financial position didn't rely on, for example, hoodwinking low-income students or harming the health of teenagers.

What the studies show is that sustainable investors can factor values into their decision making without having a completely different set of expectations for how those investments will perform or how much they will cost. For the most part, sustainable investments act just like investments of any kind—they typically perform as well as, and sometimes better than, a more standard investment, with a similar range of risk potential.

Bottom line—Performance does not need to be an impediment to the sustainable investor.

CHAPTER 5

The Ladder of Impact —or—What It Looks Like to Become a Sustainable Investor

We want you to know that sustainable investing can be simple. So many financial institutions make everything about investing seem complicated and exhausting, and we're here to just say no.

But we also like to say that sustainable investing is personal and will look a little different for everybody. So how can you make an activity that is so personal and customized more straightforward?

Here's our plan. In this chapter, we're going to start by figuring out where you are in your personal investing journey. Sustainable investing functions a little differently for people at different stages of life, so we're going to walk you through what we call the Ladder of Impact. Luckily, there are only a few rungs on that ladder.

In later chapters, we'll talk more about how you choose the investments best suited to your values, and then give you actions to take that will start you down the path—not just to making a sustainable investment, but to becoming a sustainable investor. For right now, though, the best place to start is where you already are.

For the sake of full transparency, we should point out that we're making a few assumptions about who you are and what you are doing. Such as:

- You have some financial goals—saving for a rainy day, buying a house, retiring, and so on.
- You have some money to invest—either a lump sum or smaller amounts you can invest regularly

- You want to invest—either right now or in the near future.
- You want to know enough to make good decisions, but you're not interested in a huge research project.

Sound like you? Read on.

RUNG 1—Sustainable Investing for Those Who Are Just Starting Out

The first rung of the Ladder of Impact is for the starters. At Till, we have a special place in our hearts for people who are just beginning to invest—to move beyond bank accounts and cash under the mattress. This is especially true because very few financial firms want to cater to novices who have low balances.

But we think the newbies are alright. Because if you're going to be a sustainable investor, you may as well do it from the start.

Maybe you just got your first job or a big raise, and you want to set some of that new income aside for the future. Maybe you're starting to think about some big life milestones, like buying a house or having a child. Or maybe you have a little money already—a gift from your family, say, or an inheritance—but you're just starting to think about what you want to do with it.

Now you've got to figure out what to invest in and how to make it sustainable. The key on rung 1 of the Ladder is to use sustainable investments as you transition over time from a bank saver to an investor.

Let's meet, as an example, Ashleigh. Ashleigh is an activist at heart, someone who really wants to see more women succeeding in the worlds of business and politics. She's a few years into her career and she makes a modest income doing social media work for a local business, so she doesn't have a lot of extra money to set aside. But she gives where she can—she volunteers at local women's shelters and attends political rallies on women's issues. She shops at women-owned stores and tells her friends about them.

Ashleigh is also thinking ahead. She sets aside a little money every month into an Individual Retirement Account (IRA) to save for retirement. And, she would like to start saving to one day have a down payment on a home.

Ashleigh has always seen these two activities—saving for retirement and housing, and fighting for women's rights—as independent of each other. But they don't have to be.

Let's look at where Ashleigh has her money right now:

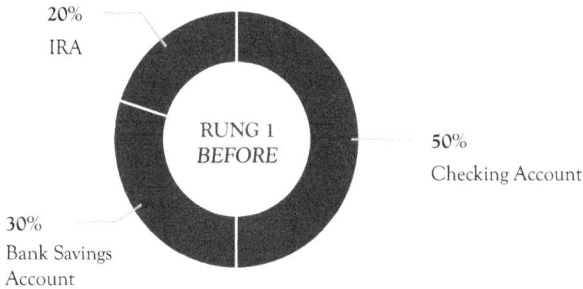

20%
IRA

RUNG 1
BEFORE

50%
Checking Account

30%
Bank Savings
Account

This is typical of someone in Ashleigh's situation—most of her money is in her checking account, as she needs it for rent, car payments, and other monthly expenses. But she has built up her savings, and her monthly contributions to her IRA are adding up as well.

However, none of her money reflects who Ashleigh is as a person and what she cares about. The question for Ashleigh is, where do you look first if you want to align your values with your money?

Let's start with the IRA. Individuals can set up an IRA with almost any mutual fund or ETF provider, and it's as easy to choose a sustainable fund as it is any other type of investment. We'll talk a lot more about making that choice in Chapter 8.

But Ashleigh doesn't need to stop there. If she wants to start setting aside money for a down payment on a house, she could also choose to open a separate account in a sustainable fund for that goal. There are numerous broad-based sustainable funds and exchange-traded funds (ETFs) that incorporate gender equity into their analysis. There are even some funds and ETFs that prioritize companies with female leadership (although those funds may be a little risky for someone in Ashleigh's shoes).

After making those changes, her money could look like this:

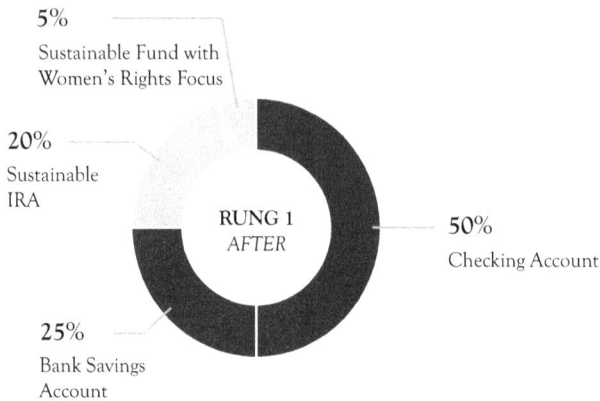

5%

Sustainable Fund with
Women's Rights Focus

20%

Sustainable
IRA

RUNG 1
AFTER

50%

Checking Account

25%

Bank Savings
Account

Now Ashleigh's investments look a little more like she does—fiscally responsible and interested in sustainability and women's rights. More importantly, Ashleigh has set herself up so that as her wealth grows, it does so in a sustainable way. As she continues to put away money in her IRA and house fund, her chart becomes more and more sustainable. In just a few years, it could look like this:

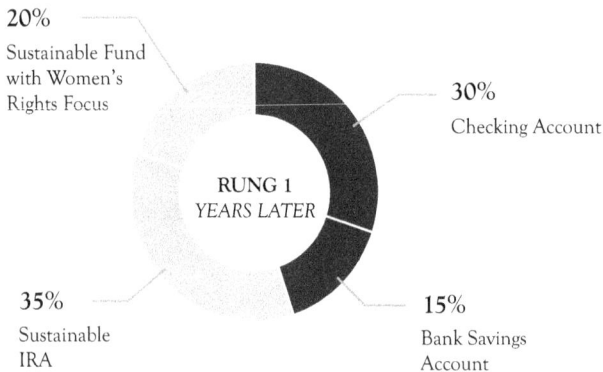

20%

Sustainable Fund
with Women's
Rights Focus

30%

Checking Account

RUNG 1
YEARS LATER

35%

Sustainable
IRA

15%

Bank Savings
Account

Building your net worth and increasing your impact on the world around you at the same time? That's what sustainable investing is all about.

An important note here is that Ashleigh didn't invest sustainably *in lieu of* having sound personal finance practices. She simply decided that, where possible, if she was going to have an investment, it should reflect her values. She did not pull all of her money out of her checking account to throw into an impact fund—nor should she. She didn't pull money out of her retirement savings because she wanted to invest in a specific green energy company. Goals, risk, and income all still matter. There's just another factor being added to the equation.

RUNG 2—Building for Sustainable Retirement, and Other Specific Goals

Look at you! You're well into your successful career, and along the way, you've been able to participate in a couple of company-sponsored retirement plans. Or maybe you like to think ahead and have been putting money into an IRA. For many people, a retirement plan is the largest asset they will compile in their lifetime, so it's a perfect vehicle for sustainable investors to use to generate impact.

At the same time, you may have picked up a couple of other accounts. Perhaps you have a 529 account to save for college for your children or grandchildren. Maybe you opened an account at a brokerage to invest in a specific company or two that you really believe in. What about that bank savings account you've had since college as a "backup" that you haven't touched in 20 years?

The key on Rung 2 is to view your growing variety of financial accounts as **opportunities** to invest sustainably. Let's look at an example.

Meet Michael and Tamara. They have three children and are especially concerned about how climate change will affect their futures. They've started to put away money for college savings for their children but want to balance that with continuing to save for retirement. Michael has moved through a couple of employers on his way up the ladder and has both an old 401(k) leftover from a prior job and an existing 401(k) with his current employer. Tamara has contributed to an IRA throughout her career. Their financial portfolio looks like this:

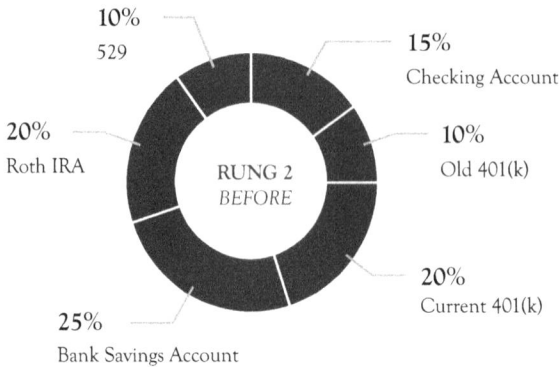

10%
529

15%
Checking Account

20%
Roth IRA

RUNG 2
BEFORE

10%
Old 401(k)

20%
Current 401(k)

25%
Bank Savings Account

All those slices of the pie are *opportunities* for sustainable investment. But as Michael and Tamara are about to find out, not all opportunities are created alike.

Who Gets to Choose?

Rung 1 of the Ladder of Impact is easy because you are always in control. If you're tossing money into a personal mutual fund account, or an IRA, you get to choose from virtually the entire mutual fund universe. You'll find hundreds of sustainable options.

But as your portfolio grows, you'll discover situations where you don't always get to choose the menu. This happens most often with **workplace retirement accounts** and **529 college savings plans**.

Workplace retirement accounts—better known as 401(k)s and 403(b)s—are set up by your employer and, as a result, your employer is the one who chooses the investment options. Similarly, 529 college savings accounts are generally sponsored by states in partnership with a financial institution, and those sponsors select the investment options.

As interest in sustainable investing has grown, many employers and 529 sponsors have included a sustainable option in their plans—often, one single option. Others have not. So if Michael and Tamara want to take advantage of all their sustainable investing opportunities, they are going to have to take inventory.

Green, Yellow, and Red

Let's take a closer look at Michael and Tamara's financial accounts. The Roth IRA is an easy green. The couple can move that account themselves into any sustainable option they choose.

There's another easy green lurking in there as well—the old 401(k) from a previous employer. While many employers allow you to keep your 401(k) accounts even after you change jobs, you are also allowed to roll that money over into an aptly named rollover IRA. Once you move the money out of the workplace retirement plan and into your own IRA, you once again can choose any sustainable option that suits you best.

The current 401(k), though, is a different story. While Michael's employer includes a dozen fund options in his 401(k) plan, only one of them is labeled "sustainable." It's a generic-looking fund that doesn't provide much detail about its approach.

We'll talk more later in the book about how to evaluate these funds. But for now, let's assume Michael and Tamara decide that they would rather include a sustainable fund in their retirement plan, even if they don't know much about it. We'll call that a yellow.

Next, they take a look at their 529 plan and discover there are no sustainable options at all. That's red.

There's one other big chunk of Michael and Tamara's financial pie they haven't looked at—their bank savings and checking accounts. It's always a good idea to keep a certain amount of money set aside for emergencies in a bank account because that money is insured by the government and is very easy to access when you need it. But in Michael and Tamara's case, their bank accounts make up 40 percent of their total savings.

Now is a great time for the couple to use some of the money in their savings to open up a personal account with a sustainable fund that genuinely scratches their climate-fighting itch—such as an ETF that focuses exclusively on clean energy stocks.

Greening Up the Portfolio

After taking advantage of all their sustainable investing opportunities, Michael and Tamara's portfolio might look like this:

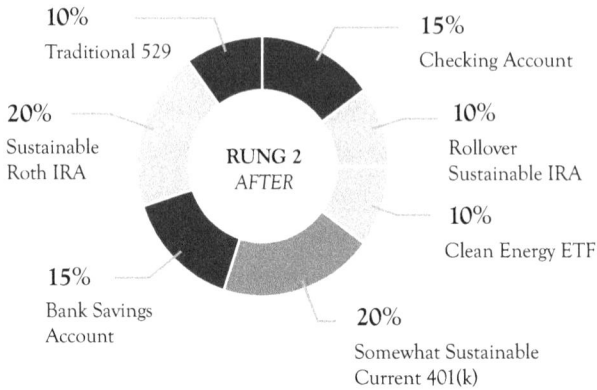

No, they don't have a fully green pie chart, but they have made tremendous strides in becoming more sustainable with their savings. They moved their money out of Michael's old 401(k) into a sustainable IRA, found a clean energy ETF that they really liked, and moved their existing IRA into a more sustainable mutual fund. They did the best they could with their existing 401(k), although they didn't have a good option for their state-sponsored 529 account.

Another important point: like Ashleigh, Michael and Tamara didn't make big changes in their personal finance strategy. They still are balancing saving for retirement and saving for college as they were before, and they still have emergency funds. The only change is they have taken the opportunities available to select sustainable funds.

Rung 3—Building a More Impactful Sustainable Portfolio

Over time, you will get to a place where you're well on your way to meeting your most pressing financial goals. You're comfortable with the amount you have saved for retirement, and those mortgage and tuition payments don't seem as onerous. If you're going to make any new investments, you'd like to ramp up your sense of impact. And maybe also, you'd like to look for opportunities in some riskier areas of the market.

Rung 3 is about adding some oomph to an existing sustainable portfolio. Once you're in a good position to meet your financial goals, how can you take your sustainable portfolio to the next level?

Among traditional portfolios, the usual advice for more seasoned investors is to diversify. Add a small-cap fund or an international fund. Look for interesting strategies and take a few risks. The same can be said of sustainable portfolios. Adding small-cap funds can help you target emerging new ideas. Non-U.S. funds can hook you up with sustainable leaders throughout the world. Thematic funds target companies that are doing the most to address an important sustainable issue.

As an example, let's meet Rodrigo and Sofia. Both of them have had long, successful careers, and they have built up a significant amount of savings in their retirement plan. In addition, they recently had an unexpected financial windfall as they inherited some money from a family member. Their only child is in college, and there is plenty of money in her 529 to support the rest of her collegiate career—and contribute to grad school, if needed.

Rodrigo and Sofia went through the process of moving all of their retirement savings into funds that are broadly sustainable and well-diversified to make sure they meet their goals for retirement. But they still have additional money sitting in a generic mutual fund and are ready to put that into funds that not only can further diversify their portfolios, but that will be more focused on what drives them individually.

Here's what their financial picture looks like currently:

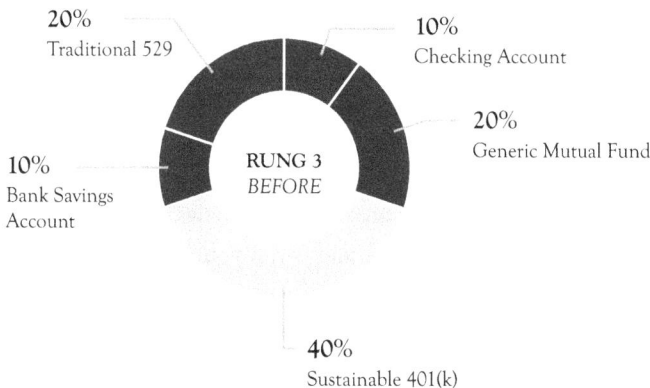

20%
Traditional 529

10%
Checking Account

20%
Generic Mutual Fund

10%
Bank Savings
Account

RUNG 3
BEFORE

40%
Sustainable 401(k)

Rodrigo and Sofia agree that they should split their generic mutual fund into two investments, one that each of them can pick. Rodrigo is passionate about technology and is a big believer not just in wind energy as a green solution but as an investment, so he decides to invest in a Wind Energy ETF. Such a concentrated position wasn't necessarily appropriate for a retirement account, but here, it is a justifiable risk.

Sofia is a fierce advocate for animal welfare and decides to put her half into a fund that divests from companies that contribute to animal suffering, either through animal testing, poor farming practices, or other means. The fund is only a few years old, but she is a believer in its methodology.

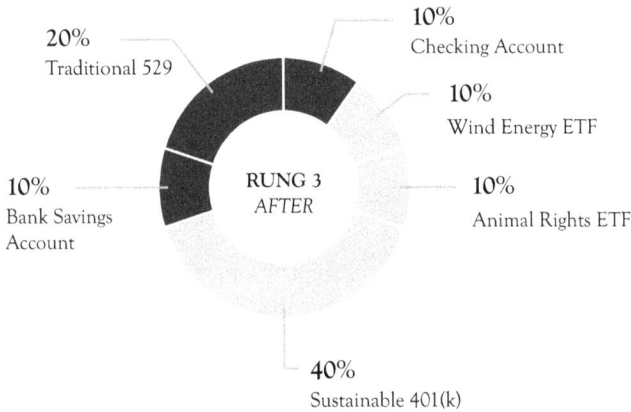

Now, they are more diversified than they were before, and their savings reflect more of what they truly care about. Moving their money out of the generic mutual fund into targeted funds has accomplished both goals at once.

In Short...

The good news about the Ladder of Impact is that there is a spot on it for you. No matter where you are in your financial life, you can focus on sustainability in the way you save and invest your money.

But how do you look through the many different sustainable funds and strategies and find one that's right for you? We think there's a way to make that task much simpler.

CHAPTER 6

The Three Fighting Styles— The Key to Finding the Right Fund for You

At the end of the day, becoming a sustainable investor comes down to picking the right fund among the hundreds of options available to you.

That sounds like a hard task, and the funds themselves aren't making it any easier. If you look at most educational material about sustainability coming from the investment industry, you'll find a messy jumble of jargon, traditional investing concepts, "theories of change," and data that even the fund companies themselves struggle to explain. You'll be asked questions like do you prefer a negative screening approach or a thematic approach?

If you're not excited about that, we're with you. And we're here to tell you—you don't need to understand the industry's explanations to succeed as a sustainable investor. Knowing yourself and what you are about is enough.

Put Your Gloves On

We've talked already about identifying the values you prioritize, and that's the right place to start. In fact, many financial industry advisors and planners put a lot of focus here, running clients through questionnaires and asking about their charities, for example.

But your causes are only one part of the equation, and there's another critical question that we don't think gets asked nearly enough: What is your fighting style?

If you're familiar with investing at all, this question may seem puzzling. It's certainly not something that comes up with traditional investing. But sustainable investing isn't just about expressing yourself—it's largely about creating change. So it makes sense to ask, how do I like to create change?

Let's say there was a business in your community that you thought was causing harm, for example, by selling alcohol or cigarettes to underage kids. If you wanted to do something about that, there are three things you might choose to do:

- **Avoid** them—that is, don't give this company your business.
- **Reward** better businesses—as in, find a competitor who is doing things right, and reward them with your business
- **Influence** the owners—which means, talk with the owners and see if you can get them to respond to your concerns

As it turns out, these three "fighting styles" are also used heavily by sustainable funds (they just call it something different). Many sustainable funds use a combination of all three styles, while others specialize in just one. And it's relatively easy to figure out which style each fund is using. In our experience, finding an approach that appeals to your fighting style is the key to figuring out what kind of sustainable fund is right for you.

Fighting Style 1: Avoiding

This fighting style, known in the industry as "divesting" or "negative screening," is simple: just don't invest in companies you disagree with. Don't like cigarettes? Refuse to invest in companies that sell them.

This fighting style says that, regardless of how you value certain aspects of sustainability, some companies are just not worth investing in at all.

Most often, this happens at an industrywide level. For many decades, some funds have divested from "sin stocks" such as alcohol or gambling, often in a nod to investors with religious motivations. In the sustainable investing world, divesting from fossil fuels is increasingly common. Other industries commonly divested from include weapons manufacturers and tobacco companies.

The divesting style has a lot going for it. The biggest pro is that it's straightforward: you either invest in this type of company or you don't. It can feel good knowing that your wealth is not coming from industries or companies that go against your values or mission.

It's also very difficult to greenwash this type of activity. We'll talk more about greenwashing later in the book, but in short, it refers to companies that claim to be sustainable without backing those claims up with action. When your strategy is as straightforward as we won't invest in X, it is very easy to see if you're not telling the truth.

In fact, there is an excellent online tool that you can use to see what funds are divested from certain industries. It's called fossilfreefunds.org, and it's managed by the sustainability resource firm As You Sow. At their site, you can look at 3,000 different funds to see how invested they are in controversial areas such as fossil fuels, weapons, tobacco, and more.

If you are currently invested in any mutual fund, look it up at fossilfreefunds.org and see how invested it is in these areas. It can be an eye-opening, and motivating, exercise to see where you're earning your money.

Another big plus for the avoiding strategy is that it's easy, and often cheap, to implement. There's not a lot of analysis or explanation demanded of funds that avoid companies in the X, Y, or Z industries. In principle, that can keep costs down.

Critics of the avoiding style point out that your impact is ultimately limited with this approach. You might not own shares of that big oil company, but someone does. Divesting makes a bold statement, but at the same time, it also removes you and your concerns from the conversation. For some people, that's ok.

What Harvard, Catholics, and Pittsburgh All Have in Common

One of the great challenges of creating change is that there's always someone who likes things just as they are—and often, those someones have lots of money, resources, and influence to fight back against change.

That's certainly been the case with climate change—fossil fuel companies have been aggressive about fending off conversations about climate realities. And one of the keys to breaking through that wall of resistance has been widespread divestment efforts.

Unsurprisingly, large U.S. colleges and universities have been among those leading the charge. Universities are an interesting force for change because they have large endowments and a knowledgeable student constituency. They have a history of using divestment programs going at least as far back as the anti-apartheid movements of the late 1980s. Divestment from fossil fuels started about a decade ago at Swarthmore. After many years of pressure, Harvard agreed to divest its $40 billion + endowment from fossil fuels in 2021.

But higher education has some company in these divestment efforts. For example, the Catholic Church has taken up the cause. Following leadership from the Global Catholic Climate Movement, hundreds of global catholic organizations have ended fossil fuel investments while pursuing the use of renewable energy.

Even many city governments have gotten involved. Around the world, 18 large cities have committed to C40's "Divesting from Fossil Fuels, Investing in a Sustainable Future" pledge, including Seattle, New York, Los Angeles, New Orleans, and Pittsburgh in the United States. The pledge calls for cities to remove fossil fuels from city investment programs and to press for changes in the pension funds of municipal workers.

If Harvard, Catholics, or Pittsburgh were engaged in these divestment efforts on their own, it might not be enough to create change. But in total, divestment efforts have moved more than $40 trillion away from the fossil fuel industry. Together, this strange group of bedfellows with a similar avoiding style make it nearly impossible for fossil-fuel companies to ignore climate change concerns.

Fighting Style 2: Rewarding

The rewarding style is about trying to identify the companies that are using sustainable practices and that are benefiting from doing so. Within the industry, this approach is often called "ESG integration." It is meant to appeal to investors who want to put their money behind the good actors—to tie their personal financial futures to investments that they believe are most likely to have a long future.

ESG integration strategies are quite numerous and highly varied. Each fund that uses a rewarding style must identify companies that are socially responsible in addition to being good financial investments. They may focus on different aspects of sustainability, or different measures of financial success. Some narrow down their investments to only 30 or 40 stocks, while others invest in hundreds of stocks. Some use a team of analysts and an in-house method of identifying sustainable companies; others use lists created by an outside group.

For investors who want to use a rewarding style, that is both a challenge and an opportunity. Because there are literally hundreds of fund options out there to choose from, there's a very good chance of finding an option that is a great fit for the things you care about most. No matter where you are in your investing life or on the Ladder of Impact, you can choose a fund that makes you comfortable as both an investor and as an advocate for sustainability.

On the other hand, there are a lot of funds to choose from. It can be a little daunting.

In Chapter 8, we're going to walk you through a short series of steps that will make it easier to sort through the volume. For now, it's enough to say that you don't have to make a *perfect* choice to start down the path of sustainable investing. There are a lot of good choices, and it's relatively easy to move money later.

But there is a dark side to the world of ESG integration: of the three styles, it is the most susceptible to greenwashing. Because there's no pre-defined understanding of what a "good" company is, fund managers can claim to be identifying sustainable companies while not actually doing so with any real rigor. No one wants to be fooled by these imposters, so we will spend Chapter 7 showing what they look like and how to weed them out.

The Surprising Factor Most Americans Consider First When Thinking About Sustainability

The fact that there is no single definition of a good, sustainable company is not necessarily a red flag. In our view, rewarding style funds are so varied because investors themselves have such varied viewpoints. Where you stand on sustainability very much depends on where you sit.

For example, climate change is regularly identified as a top priority for sustainable investors, as outlined in surveys by BlackRock and others. But JUST Capital—a nonprofit that surveys public priorities and engages in discussions with companies about them—looks beyond investors to understand the priorities of the general public. Their surveys consistently show that the public's number one sustainability concern is labor practices and policies.

The American public – liberal, conservative, high-income, low-income, men, women, young generations, and older generations –

> *has been unified in what it wants from corporate America over the six years we've conducted this survey, and that is for* **companies to put workers at the heart of just business practices***.*
> —JUST Capital, 2022

Whatever your priorities are, they're not wrong. In fact, they are your guideposts to success as a sustainable investor.

Fighting Style 3: Influencing

The influencing fighting style is all about raising your voice. Funds that apply an influencing style go beyond the investment itself and take on all opportunities to exert their influence by engaging with the companies they invest in.

Through their ownership of significant pieces of publicly traded companies, fund managers hold tremendous amounts of sway. Because of this sway, fund managers can engage with companies and pressure them to act in certain ways—through company meetings, analyst calls, and proxy votes. Some sustainable fund managers do this extensively, through actions such as:

- Raising concerns with company management
- Asking questions on analyst calls or other everyday interactions demanding action on specific issues
- Joining proxy voting movements designed to force changes in leadership or company policy

Influencing strategies have a lot of potential to drive change. When large-scale investors ask tough questions, companies look for ways to give better answers.

Proxy voting is especially potent. Once a year, every publicly held company holds a shareholder meeting to update their investors on company developments. It's also where shareholders vote on key issues facing the company. Shareholders who don't show up to the meeting can still vote on those issues by proxy.

Power by Proxy

If you have any money in a mutual fund, that mutual fund manager is using *your money* to vote for company proxies in whatever direction they see fit.

You may see in the media that BlackRock, for example, owns some significant percentage of a company, but that's not accurate. In fact, BlackRock's *clients* own that percentage of the company, and BlackRock votes on behalf of those clients. If you're invested in a BlackRock fund, you are one of those clients—they are voting *on your behalf.*

This is meant to be a convenience for investors, but it's not necessarily a great fit for a committed sustainable investor. Knowing how fund managers are voting with your money is an important part of the influencing fighting style, and it is a valuable tool for any sustainable investor.

Proxy votes are typically about high-level leadership decisions, like Board of Director elections or executive compensation plans. All of which can have implications for sustainable investors. Increasingly, though, activist shareholders have used proxy votes to force companies' hands on sustainability concerns—often against the strong objections of company management.

Just since 2020, we have seen shareholders influence companies in powerful ways, including:

- Requiring gun manufacturer Sturm Ruger to conduct a study on the impact of their products on human rights as a result of gun violence.
- Requiring FedEx to disclose more of their lobbying activities and expenditures.
- Requiring petrochemical company Phillips 66 to investigate reducing their production of single-use plastics.

The good news is that many fund managers make their Proxy Voting Guidelines available to the public. They won't always publicize the existence of these guidelines, but they have them and will share them with those who ask. If they are worth their salt, they will also post their actual votes on their website.

If this fighting style appeals to you, now is a great time to look at one of your fund managers and see if they make their proxy voting guidelines available. See how detailed it is. Compare it with the proxy vote guidelines from one of the most actively engaged sustainable fund managers out there, Domini. See if you can determine how they voted on the FedEx or Phillips 66 proxy vote in 2022. The information is out there.

It should be noted that engaging is generally not compatible with screening out companies that could be bad actors. If you divest from a company, you are giving up the power to influence them through engagement. Engagement activities are often layered on top of rewarding strategies, but not always. Some funds apply limited sustainability analysis when they invest in a company, preferring to only address sustainability issues as part of their conversations with company management.

In our experience, engagement is a tough thing for "mainstream" fund managers to navigate. If you are a fund manager who offers both sustainable funds and traditional funds, but you only get one vote on a sustainability issue at a company, how do you make that vote? How do you represent all of your clients? There's not an easy answer. So, if you're interested in engagement, you may have more luck with a company that has all of its funds focused on sustainability.

You're also unlikely to find many index funds with an engaging style, so engaging funds are usually not the cheapest option. But it may be that you find that cost to be worth it.

Engagement, and proxy voting in particular, is where the rubber meets the road for sustainable funds. It is one thing to say that you're concerned about board diversity. It's another to have to decide to vote for or against a board with little or no diversity.

A Proxy Vote Success Story: Exxon Mobile

In late 2020, a small hedge fund announced a big plan.

A newly formed hedge fund with an activist mindset, Engine No. 1, announced plans to try and seek seats on the board of directors at Exxon Mobil. The group felt that Exxon was way behind the curve when it came to climate change and needed to change course. Importantly, Engine No.1 had gotten the backing of a big player—California pension giant CalSTRS. However, there was a long way to go.

Exxon, worried about the effort to replace their chosen board members, met early and often with Engine No. 1 and went so far as to change some of their proposed board members and create a new business line "ExxonMobil Low Carbon Solutions." But it wasn't enough for Engine No. 1, who was doing its own work behind the scenes, meeting with large fund managers like Black-Rock, Vanguard, and State Street. They were making a strong case that Exxon's lack of climate change strategy was destroying value at an alarming rate.

When the time to vote came in the summer of 2021, Exxon's management came out strongly against the four directors proposed by Engine No. 1. They encouraged shareholders to vote for their proposed slate of directors. And yet:

Engine No. 1 succeeded in getting three of their four proposed candidates onto the board. They largely won over BlackRock and State Street and convinced proxy voting consultants ISS and Glass Lewis to support their candidates as well. The result was a tremendous rebuke of Exxon management by shareholders—and a big win for the sustainable investing community.

In Short...

The fighting styles are useful because they are grounded in the ways that people think about taking action and driving change, not just in the investment world but in all walks of life. And as we repeatedly say, being a successful sustainable investor is all about knowing what you care about.

You may find that you are very specifically attracted to one style or another. Or maybe, you naturally gravitate to a mix of different styles. That's all fine because funds are like that too. Some are only interested in divestment, for example, others use a mix of all three styles. When it comes time to go shopping for a specific fund for yourself, you'll be able to tell pretty quickly which style a fund uses and whether that's a fit for you.

But before you start picking out your sustainable investments, we want to make sure you eliminate the not-serious funds from consideration. We want to make you a great greenwashing detective.

CHAPTER 7

How to Be a Great Greenwashing Detective

We've talked a lot about how funds identify sustainable companies and what they do with that analysis in the last few chapters. In a perfect world, these funds would then be perfectly transparent about their process and give you lots of information about what they do, why they do it, and how effective it is. But this is not a perfect world, and there is a very important challenge we need to acknowledge before we find your sustainable investing fit.

It's called greenwashing.

Greenwashing happens when companies or funds promote themselves as sustainable without any real substance to back it up. Unfortunately, it's pretty common among companies who want to hit on the hot trends while sweeping their less attractive activities under the rug. Just in 2022, large firms including BNY Mellon and Deutsche Bank have been investigated by regulators over greenwashing issues.

But funds and ETFs can greenwash too.

The Many Shades of Greenwashing

Not all greenwashing is alike, and not every company that is accused of greenwashing is a hopeless investment. One aspect of becoming a great greenwashing detective is recognizing how severe of a problem the greenwashing is. Here's a handy guide.

Scale of Greenwashing:

	By Companies
Light greenwashing	Companies that *aim* to be good corporate citizens but don't fully recognize the harm they might be responsible for. For example, a clothing company not knowing or caring how their suppliers treat their workers.
Standard greenwashing	Companies that talk a good game on sustainability, but don't follow through. For example, a supermarket chain that claims to be a good employer while paying substandard salaries.
Heavy greenwashing	Companies that intentionally distract from clearly unsustainable practices. For example, an oil company claiming to be green.

	By Funds
Light greenwashing	Funds that genuinely *intend* to use a sustainable approach. But they lack a consistent strategy, aren't transparent about their efforts, and/or don't communicate clearly about what impact an investor can expect from their investment.
Standard greenwashing	Funds that modestly reposition existing investment strategies, then promote those changes as evidence of a "green" approach.
Heavy greenwashing	Funds that offer no clear sustainability strategy but use misleading marketing to attract sustainable investors.

When funds greenwash, they put a lot of focus on their labeling. They will call their investments "green," "sustainable," or "ESG" without having a meaningful sustainable strategy. In some cases, these offenders are relatively easy to identify. Other times, the problem becomes one of transparency—that is, you just can't tell from any of their reports or documents just what they are doing at all.

Even traditional funds are rarely as transparent as you would like about their processes. How can you confidently chart a path as a sustainable investor in such an uncertain environment?

Greenwashers Aren't Very Good at It

Here's the good news: While there are certainly fund managers who greenwash, the reality is that they're not very good at it. You can be a great **Greenwashing Detective** by asking just two basic questions when looking at any fund.

> Question 1: Do they say what they do?
>
> Question 2: Do they do what they say?

We're going to show you how to answer these fundamental questions so that you can feel good about what you're investing in, while also having as clear a sense as possible of what fund managers are doing with your money. We are going to look at three sustainable funds as examples to help you understand where to look, and how to interpret what you see.

These funds include an ESG exchange-traded index fund (ETF) from BlackRock, an actively managed ESG fund from Calvert, and an actively managed ESG fund from Goldman Sachs. They are all marketed as sustainable core equity funds, meaning they are all suitable for the typical long-term investor. They don't have a particular theme or focus beyond general sustainability, so we can easily compare them and use them as examples for evaluating other funds.

All of the information in this analysis was pulled from the fund managers' websites in December 2022.

Question 1: Do they say what they do?

What to look for: How the fund defines sustainability and what they do about it.

Where to look: Fund Fact Sheet; ESG information from the website; Proxy Voting Guidelines; Principal Investment Strategies in the Summary Prospectus

What to look out for: Heavy use of the word "proprietary," little discussion of strategy beyond a description of "ESG," flimsy proxy voting guidelines.

The starting point: the Fund's Fact Sheet

Virtually every fund offers a "fact sheet," which is a quick summary of high-level fund information about its returns, risk profile, fees, and holdings. You're likely to only get a sentence or two about the fund's strategy and how it addresses sustainability factors, but those sentences are a good starting point. Let's take a look at a couple of examples.

BlackRock iShares MSCI USA ESG Select ETF

Fact Sheet Says: "The iShares MSCI USA ESG Select ETF seeks to track the investment results of an index composed of U.S. companies that have positive environmental, social, and governance characteristics as identified by the index provider."

What this means to us: This is a fund that uses an outside provider MSCI (Morgan Stanley Capital International) for sustainability research. And, this fund uses a "rewarding" fighting style, investing in "good" companies according to MSCI. If you want, you can do some additional research about MSCI to better understand what they consider sustainable.

Calvert Equity Fund

Fact Sheet Says: "The investment team applies a fundamental approach to investing ... The Calvert Principles for Responsible Investment (Calvert Principles) provide a framework for the evaluation of ESG factors and guide our active engagement efforts with company management teams."

What this means to us: Calvert uses their own in-house methodology for evaluating sustainability, and we will want to look at these Calvert Principles for more. They also clearly use an "engaging" fighting style.

Goldman Sachs U.S. Equity ESG Fund

Fact Sheet Says: The team builds the portfolio one company at a time by ... assessing a company's balance sheet, earnings and cash flows with a focus on material ESG factors. In considering ESG factors, the team applies a proprietary approach that goes beyond third party ESG scores. This proprietary approach to ESG integration is a hallmark of the strategy.

What this means to us: This is an ESG integrator, but it is clear from the beginning that they are not planning to tell you very much about how they define sustainability or what their fighting style is.

The Next Step: Follow the Trail

A good fund fact sheet will give you a good idea of where to go to learn more about the fund's sustainability strategy. Let's follow the trail of our three funds.

BlackRock iShares MSCI USA ESG Select ETF—MSCI ESG Ratings Website

What we see: It's clear that MSCI has made a significant commitment to ESG analysis by the depth and breadth of content they make public about their ratings. While their approach may not appeal to everyone, they certainly provide a lot of insight into their process, including technical detail.

What this means to us: We can feel pretty good that there isn't greenwashing going on here. Our questions now can be more about how we feel about the process—do we agree with what they consider important, how they pick "winners" and "losers," and if that lines up with what we are looking for.

Calvert Equity Fund—Calvert Principles for Responsible Investment

What we see: Calvert's principles are much simpler than MSCI's and fit in a single two-page document. They clearly lay out what they consider to be "good" and "bad," and they suggest that they both reward good companies and avoid bad ones.

What this means to us: Calvert treats sustainability as a company-wide effort. They start with how they see themselves as a company—a "global leader in Responsible Investing"—and let their funds' methodologies follow that. There's enough detail to get a strong feel for what they will focus on with your investment dollars.

Goldman Sachs U.S. Equity ESG Fund—Summary Prospectus

What we see: Summary prospectuses are mandated by the SEC, as a more "readable" companion to the longer and more unwieldy "Prospectus." We can't enthusiastically recommend reading a summary prospectus for every fund you are interested in, because they are generally written in legal-ese. However from a sustainability standpoint, the only section you need to look at is called the "Principal Investment Strategy" (or something similar). In many cases, this relatively short section can give you a lot of insight.

Sometimes you have to look at the summary prospectus if the fund isn't being particularly transparent in its fact sheet or other marketing materials. That's certainly true for this fund. And interestingly, the principal strategies section still tells us very little. The fund can generally exclude what it deems bad actors, but otherwise there is no guidance around what the fund manager considers to be important from an ESG perspective.

What this means to us: If we were a little concerned that the fact sheet wasn't very transparent about how Goldman Sachs considers sustainability, now we have some red flags going up. Not only does this give us very little insight, but the insight it does give—how the fund avoids bad actors—doesn't line up with the fact sheet. Inconsistent messaging is a bad sign.

Finally: Tell Me How You're Going to Vote

As discussed in the Fighting Styles chapter, there is a lot of value in looking at a fund's proxy voting record. Regardless of your strategy, proxy votes are a visible way to act on the principles you claim to support—a binary "yes" or "no" for fund managers to take a stand on sustainable issues that come up for a vote.

Fortunately, most fund companies provide Proxy Vote Guidelines (although you may have to call to request them). They are an excellent place to investigate a company's commitment to sustainability.

These guidelines can often be long. We recommend looking for one or two issues to compare across funds. For this exercise, we're going to focus on Board Diversity—an important issue because all shareholders vote for or against board members. Let's see what we can find.

BlackRock—U.S. Proxy Vote Guidelines

Here in the United States, regarding board diversity, BlackRock says that "We believe boards should aspire to 30 percent diversity of membership and encourage companies to have at least two directors on their board who identify as female and at least one who identifies as a member of an underrepresented group."

What this means to us: There is a lot of noncommittal language in here about what they "believe" a company should "aspire" to and what they "encourage" companies to do. BlackRock appears to be trying to leave themselves a lot of room to vote on either side of this issue, which is not surprising given that BlackRock is trying to serve both sustainable and traditional investors alike with these guidelines.

Calvert: Global Proxy Vote Guidelines

Calvert says that they will broadly "oppose individual directors ... if the board lacks at least two women and at least two people of color, and if collectively, the board is not at least 40 percent diverse."

What this means to us: This is a lot more prescriptive than the Black-Rock document. While Calvert leaves themselves some wiggle room, they are much more specific about what they will do if a board does not meet their diversity requirements. Their requirements are also stricter than BlackRock's, which is expected of a company with a sustainability focus.

Goldman Sachs: Global Proxy Voting Policy

In the United States, Goldman says that they will "Vote AGAINST or WITHHOLD from members of the Nominating Committee ... if the board does not have at least 10 percent women directors and at least one other diverse board director."

What this means to us: Goldman has the strictest language of all of our fund providers in terms of not giving any wiggle room for their voters but also has the lowest requirements for what they consider to be diverse. They are also managing the balance of different customer needs like BlackRock but with a different approach.

Three Very Different Results

In exploring this question, we've begun to come to some helpful conclusions on our three funds.

- The **BlackRock** fund delegates all the sustainability methodology to MSCI, which details a robust process. But BlackRock's proxy vote guidelines aren't very prescriptive.
- The **Calvert** fund does everything in house, so we are leaning heavily on their reputation as a sustainable investment leader. But they will take strong stands for sustainability in their voting process.
- The **Goldman Sachs** fund gives us very little detail on their process, which is a major concern, and their voting guidelines are the least sustainable of our three candidates.

Question 2: Do they do what they say?

What to look for: Commentary, with examples, of how the fund executes their sustainability strategy

Where to look: Fund fact sheets, performance commentaries, proxy vote results, and impact reports

What to look out for: A lack of details or follow-through, questionable claims with little evidence.

As a sustainable investor, you are investing in a process. At the end of the day, you want proof that the process has been followed.

All funds put out regular information about what they are invested in—fact sheets, quarterly commentaries, semiannual reports, web pages with fund statistics, and the like—and there are substantial regulations that guide it. And yet, for sustainable and traditional funds alike, there is a lot of variety in terms of the depth, quality, and clarity of that reporting. Poor or hard-to-understand reporting can be a sign of a bad investment in general, but that's particularly true of sustainable funds. That's why it's worth spending a little time looking at a fund's reporting.

Not many people enjoy reading financial reports, and that's fair. But you don't have to read that much, or have any special financial knowledge, to make good judgments about how legitimate a sustainable fund is. Gut reactions can be pretty reliable, as they are a sign that the fund doesn't speak to you or your values. Let's see how our three fund managers report on their activities to show you what we mean.

Back to the Start: Fund Fact Sheet

When we first looked at the fact sheet, we were interested in what the fund said about its investment process. Now, we're looking at the results of that process—specifically, where the fund invests its money.

BlackRock iShares MSCI USA ESG Select ETF

This BlackRock offering is an exchange-traded fund designed to track an index of companies with high MSCI ESG ratings. You can be pretty sure the fund is doing what it says it's doing, because the structure of the fund doesn't leave a lot of wiggle room.

But there is value in looking at the top holdings and sectors of the fund, to get a feel for what that MSCI index is leading you toward. The fact sheet shows that Microsoft and Apple and Alphabet are all top holdings, while Tesla also makes an appearance. Overall, the fund is heavy on technology and light on energy, which makes sense given the MSCI rating system.

What this means to us: This fund isn't a greenwashing candidate because they are clear about their approach, and there is no reason to suspect that they aren't tracking the MSCI index. You can decide that this strategy doesn't suit you, but it is a legitimate sustainable investment.

TOP HOLDINGS (%)	
Microsoft Corp	4.84
Apple, Inc	4.79
Tesla, Inc	2.26
Alphabet, Inc Class A	2.08
Home Depot, Inc	1.82
Pepsico, Inc	1.72
Texas Instrument, Inc	1.58
Automatic Data Processing, Inc	1.58
Kellogg	1.57
NVIDIA Corp	1.39
	23.63%

Holdings are subject to change.

TOP SECTORS (%)	
Information Technology	29.35
Health Care	12.77
Financials	11.09
Consumer staples	9.84
Industrials	9.51
Consumer Discretionary	8.85
Communication	5.96
Energy	3.30
Real Estate	3.53
Materials	3.19
Utilities	1.36
Cash and/or Derivatives	0.26

Calvert Equity Fund

Calvert's fact sheet reports their top-10 holdings, and there are some uncommon names in the mix. It's hard to tell from this list what criteria they are using, exactly, to choose these companies, but there's nothing here to raise eyebrows.

What this means to us: For a fund like this one, where analysts actively pick stocks with specific criteria in mind, it's common to see a wide range of companies show up in the holdings. This doesn't look like greenwashing, but we may want to dig further to see evidence of why Calvert believes they should be there.

TOP 10 HOLDINGS (%)	
Danaher Corp	4.83
Thermo Fisher Scientific, Inc	4.53
Alphabet, Inc - CL C	4.38
Visa, Inc	4.37
Microsoft Corp	4.33
MasterCard, Inc	4.15
Verisk Analytics, Inc	3.84
TJX Cos, Inc	3.62
Dollar General Corp	3.25
American Tower Corp	3.19

Goldman Sachs U.S. Equity ESG Fund

Good luck making sense of this fund's fact sheet, which is a large, consolidated document with a lot of performance data jammed on the page. You can fund more information on the fund's web page (www.gsam.com/content/gsam/us/en/advisors/fund-center/fund-finder/gs-u-s--equity-esg-fund.html), which shows some similar holdings to both of the funds above.

What this means to us: There's nothing obviously suspicious in this list of holdings, but again, it would help to see what Goldman says about how and why they select these companies to invest in.

TOP HOLDINGS (%)

01	Microsoft Corp	7.2
02	Apple, Inc	6.5
03	Eli Lilly & Co	3.8
04	Alphabet, Inc	3.7
05	NextEra Energy, Inc	3.3
06	Procter & Gamble Co	3.2
07	JPMorgan Chase & CO	3.2
08	Danaher Corp	3.0
09	CVS Health Corp	3.0
10	Bristol-Myers Squibb Co	2.9

How did the process play out?
Performance Commentaries

At their best, performance commentaries give you some of the best insight into the ongoing discussions being held by a fund's management team and can give you important insights into why and how they make their decisions. That this is much more relevant for active funds (like our Calvert and Goldman Sachs examples) than it is for passive funds (like the BlackRock fund) where the decisions are being dictated by an index.

BlackRock—n/a

One of the limitations of index funds like this one is that they often don't provide much in the way of regular reporting about specific holdings in the portfolio. You must have faith in how the MSCI index is constructed. Or you can look at the firm's impact report, which we will discuss in a moment.

Calvert Equity Fund Quarterly Commentary

Calvert gives a lot of information about the noteworthy stocks in their fund, including why they performed the way they did and why they like them from both a financial and sustainable perspective. For example, in the quarterly commentary we reviewed, they mention that Dollar General has "many locations representing the only convenient general merchandise storefront for miles," which support the company's shares and that wireless infrastructure provider American Tower "provides a mission critical service in today's increasingly digital economy," making the company a good candidate for growth.

What this means to us: Seeing actual examples of sustainable considerations driving investment decisions is what we are looking for, and Calvert provides exactly that here. You won't see this for every holding in the portfolio; a couple of strong examples are as good as you can hope for. It's clear that Calvert is using their sustainability methodology as advertised.

Goldman Sachs: Quarterly Commentary

Goldman talks in detail about the best and worst performing stocks in their portfolio. But oddly, there is almost no discussion of how sustainability issues are factoring into their decision making. Goldman's commentaries are not alone in this—a lot of supposed sustainable funds say almost nothing about how they apply their strategy. Is that because they can't be bothered to tell you, or because they don't really know?

What this means for us: Red flags continue to go up in our analysis of this fund. First, the company was unwilling to tell us how they considered sustainability factors. Then, their description of their strategy didn't line up with their marketing materials. Now, their fund performance review barely mentions sustainability, despite "ESG" being in the name of the fund. It is very difficult, if not impossible, to see how sustainability is being factored into this strategy.

I Know What You Did Last Proxy Season... Vote Reports

Fund companies are required to document the proxy voting they do on your behalf and then make that disclosure available to investors. But some make their votes easier to find than others, and sometimes you specifically need to request the vote records.

We think it's worth it. Voting records can be long, but you can usually pick out one or two votes to look at after just a quick scan.

For example, because each of our three funds owned Alphabet in late 2022, let's see how they voted on that firm's sustainability issues. At Alphabet this year, there were votes on issues ranging from climate lobbying to misinformation to board diversity.

BlackRock

BlackRock provides "voting bulletins" for their most significant votes, including one for their votes at Alphabet. In these bulletins, they reveal and explain their votes for some, but not all, of the issues presented at the annual meeting. Here, they reveal that they voted in favor of resolutions related to water risk, diversity, and misinformation. However, they don't reveal how they voted on issues related to climate lobbying, climate change, or data collection and privacy.

What this means for us: We saw earlier how BlackRock was trying to play both sides of the sustainability coin in their voting guidelines. Not making all their votes easily accessible is another sign of this. This is understandable—they are in the unenviable position of trying to serve clients with widely opposing views on issues like climate change. For us, their lack of reporting on votes about climate change means that we can't be sure they will be voting in a way that aligns with our interests.

Calvert

A recent Calvert "Proxy Voting Dashboard" detailed all of their votes at the Alphabet annual meeting and gave a brief rationale for each of their votes. They showed that they voted "FOR" nearly every sustainability proposal, except for two: One, against the report on misinformation because they felt it was overly broad and should be conducted by an outside entity, and two, against an "Environmental Sustainability Board Committee," because they felt that Alphabet was already doing well on environmental goals and oversight.

What this means for us: We like that Calvert is transparent about every vote they make and gives a rationale for each vote as well. As for the votes themselves, we are unsurprised to see a heavy lean toward sustainability, and the two "no" votes are well-explained. Overall, this is in line with what we would expect from a sustainability-focused fund manager.

Goldman Sachs

Unlike BlackRock and Calvert, Goldman Sachs reports that they vote differently depending on which fund you're invested in. For their U.S. ESG fund, they voted *against* most of the sustainability-related proposals, including against a report on racial and gender board diversity, as well as against a report on lobbying policies. They did vote for reports on climate change and water risk and for the report on misinformation.

What this means for us: It's potentially positive that Goldman votes differently for its ESG fund than for its traditional funds (some of their nonsustainable funds voted against every single sustainable proposal). It eliminates the "playing both sides" issues that many large fund companies have to navigate. However, it's surprising that even with their ESG focus, they still voted against several sustainable proposals, and provided no rationale for their votes. It's hard to understand how Goldman considers sustainability in the process of casting these votes.

Bonus Materials: Impact Reports

While not all managers issue Impact Reports, it's worth looking to see if one is available, especially if you are interested in an index fund. Impact Reports are unusual for individual funds, but the ones that exist typically try to quantify some sustainability metrics about the holdings in the fund. It's more common to find an Impact Report for the fund company as a whole. Those reports contain more discussion about engagement activities and specific investments in sustainable companies.

For our three funds, BlackRock does report some "sustainability characteristics" that try to quantify the amount of carbon saved and industries avoided, as well as significant companywide impact reporting. Calvert provides similar data on their "Impact Metric Fact Sheet" and also issues an extensive annual Impact Report. Goldman Sachs does not report any impact information at the fund level but does release an annual Investment Stewardship report.

Because there is no standardization or regulation around Impact Reports, companies are able to pick and choose what they report on (and what they leave out). They are more marketing material than factual reporting, and it's tough to rely on them when making investments. But to be fair, some companies put meaningful effort into their impact reports, providing useful quantitative and qualitative information as well as case studies of their impacts. They can round out your understanding of a sustainable fund, but take them with a grain of salt.

In Short...

Now that we've asked and answered our two questions—do they say what they do, and do they do what they say—what can we say about our three funds?

- The **BlackRock** fund delegates all of the sustainability methodology to MSCI, which details a robust process, and the process is reflected in the holdings of the fund. But BlackRock's proxy vote guidelines aren't very prescriptive, and they aren't very transparent about how they make all their votes.
- The **Calvert** fund does everything in house, so we are leaning heavily on their reputation as a sustainable investment leader and what they tell us about their process. Fortunately, their description of their holdings and their decision-making process gives us great insight into how sustainability plays a role in the construction of their fund. Finally, they will take strong stands for sustainability in their voting process and report back on how and why they vote the way they do.
- The **Goldman Sachs** fund gives us very little detail on their process, which is a major concern, and there is very little evidence that they actually incorporate sustainable themes into their investment decisions. Their voting guidelines are

the least sustainable of our three candidates, and even though they vote differently from the rest of Goldman as a sustainable fund, they still don't vote as you would expect for a fund with an ESG label.

In other words, we've found two companies that convince us that there isn't greenwashing going on and one that didn't do that at all. Perhaps it will not surprise you to learn that, in December of 2022, Goldman Sachs agreed to pay $4 million to settle a regulatory investigation into greenwashing. In fact, the fund has some of the hallmarks of heavy greenwashing as we described earlier. It wasn't created as a sustainable fund; it was originally named the "Blue Chip" fund and operated for years with a standard large-cap strategy. Only in June of 2020 was it renamed with an "ESG" label and advertised as a sustainable fund, without much public information about whether, or how, its strategy had changed.

When we say that fund managers are not very good at greenwashing, this is what we mean. Doing a little bit of looking under the hood at Goldman revealed a significant lack of detail and follow through on any sort of ESG strategy. By being a discerning customer, and asking basic questions, it's easy to avoid greenwashing companies.

And in the process, you're going to learn a lot about the funds that don't greenwash. Our little exercise here revealed a lot about the Calvert and BlackRock funds, and we can use that information along with regular financial data like performance and fees to make an informed decision about which funds are right for us.

If there is one takeaway from this chapter, and perhaps one takeaway from this book as a whole, it is this: You can invest sustainably, and you don't need to be a financial wizard to do so. If you are willing to ask basic questions, you can find a fund that you can feel good about investing in. In the next chapter, we're going to tell you some stories about how to go about it.

CHAPTER 8

Making the Move to Sustainable Funds

Now that you have developed a good sense of what you are looking for in a sustainable fund, we'd like to tell you that there is a foolproof screening system to match your preferences to the right fund for you.

There isn't.

For most sustainable investors, this is the hardest part about taking action—narrowing down the list of options to something that suits your needs and fits easily in your portfolio (or, if you're a new investor, the portfolio you want to build). Part of the reason this is tricky is that what you want from a sustainable fund is only part of the equation. You also have to consider issues like:

- What funds are easy for me to access?
- Is this fund targeting a level of risk and return that I am comfortable with?
- Am I okay with the fees for this fund?

It's easy to get buried trying to sort through these many considerations. We know we've explored lots of different methodologies to find the simplest way from point A to point B. And it turns out the best approach we've found is to start with what you know and go from there.

Good Starting Points

1. *Look to your current providers.* Our favorite starting point is to look at your current providers. Most investors access mutual funds through one of three channels:
   - With a "brand name" mutual fund or ETF provider, for example, Vanguard or BlackRock.

- Through a brokerage account, often one that has a mutual fund platform, like Fidelity or Schwab.
- Via a workplace retirement account, typically with a limited menu of investment options.

In all three cases, your first step can be to look up what that provider offers, if anything, in terms of sustainable fund options. If you like the provider enough to be invested with them in the first place, then swapping in their sustainable products (or a sustainable product from their platform) is an easy and excellent way to get the ball rolling.

This is a solid first step, but it may not be the last step you'll want to take as a sustainable investor. We would still recommend that you take a close look at the sustainable fund you choose, to make sure it suits your values and fighting style. Keep an eye on their reporting. Are they doing what they say they will do? If not, you might eventually want to look for an upgrade.

But what if you don't have any current providers? Or you don't like the sustainable options they offer?

2. *Look to the fund profiles in the appendix of this book.* Descriptions of funds and fund companies aren't always tailored to the interests of sustainable investors. So we set out to make something a bit more useful, using input from investors and the sustainable community. We're not trying to rate them or decide which ones are good or bad—our aim is to boil down a wide range of information to something that is easy to make sense of quickly.

Our list of profiles isn't meant to be comprehensive. Consider them to be a first pass. We intend to post these profiles to our website and update/expand them over time. Using them, you'll be able to identify which companies are most closely aligned with the kind of impact you want to make. But you will need to carefully consider whether any given fund offering suits your financial needs—that is, your views of risk, return, and cost.

What if you want to look at a lot of options, to get a better understanding of what's available?

3. *Use online tools as guideposts.* As we said, there are no *foolproof* screening systems, but that doesn't mean there aren't screeners you can

access to learn more about the hundreds of sustainable funds out there. They won't give you exactly what you're looking for, but they can be helpful in identifying the big names and primary fund providers. However, you will often need to go beyond what they show you to get at the heart of a fund's strategy.

Morningstar offers an online search tool. As You Sow's tools are informative. Brokerage firms like Fidelity and Schwab have ESG criteria in their screening tools. US SIF has a free tool (using Bloomberg data) on their site. And you can always use the ultimate online tool, Google, for sustainable fund ideas—financial publications like Kiplinger's and Forbes often post lists of their favorite ESG funds based on some criteria or another. Google can be particularly helpful if you are looking for thematic funds focused on a particular issue.

These tools don't necessarily make it easy to choose a specific fund that suits you. But they do provide a good starting point to help you understand what's out there.

The Shortlist

You might have noticed in this book so far that we haven't talked about finding the "perfect" fund. That's because we don't think that's the right perspective. Everything about sustainable investing is expected to improve over time—better funds, using better data, and to drive better impact. Taking action today isn't about making a lifetime commitment to the best fund out there. It's more about understanding your options, picking one that fits what you're looking for, and keeping an eye out for new choices down the line.

Using the aforementioned starting points to create a solid shortlist will make the comparison process manageable. When creating your shortlist, find funds that broadly match what you're looking for, but don't be afraid to include something unfamiliar as well. Boil your shortlist down to about three to five funds, and don't worry about trying to make them perfect. Now that you know what you are looking for, you can be confident that your shortlist will contain a good set of options.

A Running List of Things We Don't Like About Sustainable Fund Screens

When you're creating your shortlist, you can decide to look at the bevy of ESG fund screeners offered by Morningstar, US SIF, Fidelity, or others. It's not a bad starting point, but it's useful to recognize that there are limitations to these tools. For example:

1. Their criteria are not your criteria.
2. They rely on data that isn't standardized.
3. The ESG market changes often, and not all screeners do a good job of keeping up.
4. Most screeners use a lot of confusing jargon to explain how funds are categorized.
5. Screeners don't address your personal fighting style at all.

Although we expect sustainable fund screeners to get better over time, it's worth remembering that screening tools rely to a very large degree on the way the financial industry thinks about sustainability. Until we see better evidence that their perspective is more closely aligned with the view of the sustainable investor, we'd suggest using these tools mainly for research purposes.

Let's see a few examples of how using these starting points to create a manageable shortlist might simplify the transition to becoming a sustainable investor.

Example 1: Andre's Old Retirement Fund

Andre has money in an old 401(k) with Vanguard. He would like to stay with Vanguard if possible, so he's focused on Vanguard's sustainable fund options.

He wants something with low risk and preferably low fees, which means he is probably looking at a broad-based index fund or ETF, something that focuses on large, established companies.

Andre cares about the climate and employee relations, and he wants to be in a fund that addresses those in some way.

Andre's Action Plan

Andre is going to start by looking at what Vanguard offers in terms of a broad-based sustainability fund and see if those options are helpful. As our profile shows, Vanguard isn't the most out front in terms of innovative sustainability strategies, but it does provide several options that are moderate risk and low fee.

Vanguard offers four low-fee sustainable options: An international fund, a bond fund, and two U.S.-based funds. Andre decides he's going to start with these. The international fund is labeled as high risk, and the bond fund doesn't do much for employee rights, but Andre thinks the two U.S.-based funds could be good fits.

For comparison, Andre is also going to look at a fund from one sustainable-only provider and one traditional provider from our fund profiles. For the sustainable-only provider, he decides to use the Calvert U.S. Large Cap Core Responsible Index Fund, because, while its fees are higher than the Vanguard funds, they are lower than the other funds from the sustainable-only providers. For the traditional providers, he's going to look at BlackRock's iShares ESG Aware MSCI USA ETF, as he is familiar with the BlackRock name and their fees are almost as low as Vanguard's.

Andre's Shortlist

iShares ESG Aware MSCI USA ETF

Calvert U.S. Large Cap Core Responsible Index Fund

Vanguard ESG U.S. Stock ETF

Vanguard FTSE Social Index Fund

Andre was most interested in climate concerns and employee relations. His Vanguard funds were both passive funds that largely employed an avoiding strategy that excludes companies including oil and gas companies. They also screen out companies that have global labor and human rights concerns, but they don't appear to do much to fight for better wages or working conditions here in the United States. The BlackRock fund he looked at also employed an avoiding strategy.

The Calvert U.S. Large Cap Core Responsible Index Fund was attractive, as it not only divested from bad actors but also had additional, stricter filters. Additionally, he liked that at the companies that the fund was invested in, they voted strongly to address climate and inequality issues. However, the price of the fund—the fees were nearly four times the Vanguard fund—was a concern, and there were going to be a lot of steps to get his money into the fund from his Vanguard account.

At the end, Andre decided to go with the Vanguard ESG U.S. Stock ETF. It was a broad fund with a very low fee, and it was very easy to access with his money already in Vanguard. It may not have ticked every box he wanted from a sustainability perspective, but for where he is on the impact ladder today, this is a good match.

Example 2: Sofia's Big Bonus

Sofia has some extra money in her bank savings account as a result of a recent bonus. She has a brokerage account with Fidelity that she can move her money into.

Sofia wants to invest it in something she is passionate about: wind energy. She wants to be very focused on wind energy only.

Sofia understands such a specific investment will likely carry high risk, but as she already has an established core portfolio for retirement, she is willing to accept that. She doesn't have a particular aspect of wind energy that she cares about, so she wants a fund that simply invests in wind energy companies.

Sofia's Action Plan

Sofia will explore Fidelity's platform to find wind energy funds and ETFs, and choose one to add as a supplement to her portfolio.

Sofia is going to try and stay with her current provider, Fidelity, as she looks for an investment in wind energy. She googles "wind energy mutual funds" and two pop up: The First Trust Global Wind Energy ETF and the Global X Wind Energy ETF. Both of them are available on Fidelity's platform, so Sofia is going to start with these two as her shortlist. Looking at our fund profiles, she also sees that Fidelity offers an "Environment and Alternative Energy Fund," which she will also put on her shortlist. It isn't specifically focused on wind energy, but she wants to consider broadening her impact focus.

Sofia's Shortlist

> First Trust Global Wind Energy ETF
>
> Global X Wind Energy ETF
>
> Fidelity Environment and Alternative Energy Fund

Sofia decided to start by comparing her two Wind Energy ETFs and found a few things that stood out. First, while they held largely the same companies, the Global X fund held far fewer companies. That meant more risk, Sofia knew. She also saw that the First Trust Global fund had been in existence for over 10 years, while Global X was less than three years old. Finally, over the last year, the First Trust Global fund had performed significantly better than the Global X fund. Sofia decided that if she was going to choose a pure Wind Energy ETF, she would choose the First Trust Global fund.

She also learned, in looking at the Wind Energy ETFs, that they don't only invest in wind energy. They will invest in a company that derives a significant amount of their revenues from wind energy, but they can be active in other areas as well. That made her more open to the Fidelity Alternative Energy fund.

However, when looking at the Fidelity Alternative Energy fund, she was very surprised to see some of the biggest holdings in the fund—their biggest holding was Microsoft. She didn't consider Microsoft to be an "Alternative Energy" company and was concerned that there was greenwashing going on with the fund—or at the least, that it was using a strategy that didn't make sense to her.

Therefore, she decided to stick with her initial choice, the First Trust Global Wind Energy ETF. She put her bonus money into her Fidelity account and invested it in the ETF.

Example 3: Dan and Sharon's Portfolio Puzzle Piece

Dan and Sharon have a portion of their portfolio invested in an emerging markets mutual fund through their account at Charles Schwab.

Dan and Sharon are big believers in the power of sustainable investing to change companies that they invest in, and so they have a strong preference for funds with an engaging focus and detailed proxy vote guidelines. They are willing to pay higher fees for a fund with strong engagement practices.

Dan and Sharon's financial advisor strongly suggests that they stay in an emerging markets fund as a way to diversify their holdings and manage risk in their portfolio.

Dan and Sharon's Action Plan

Dan and Sharon will research fund screeners to find emerging markets-focused ESG Funds. When they do, they will look at what the fund manager says about their engagement practices, ask for impact reports, and request proxy vote guidelines. They will prefer a fund with easy access through their Schwab account.

Dan and Sharon begin their search for an Emerging Markets ESG fund on the Schwab platform but struggled with their online tools to filter down to what they were looking for. Looking at our fund manager profiles, they like Domini's strong engagement practices, and they see on the Domini website that they offer several international funds that, while not specifically Emerging Markets, are of interest to them. They decide to include the Domini International Opportunities Fund on their shortlist.

Looking elsewhere, they go to the USSIF fund chart. There they see two Emerging Markets funds on the list: the Amana Developing World Fund and the Calvert Emerging Markets Equity Fund. They decide to put these two funds on their shortlist as well. For comparison, they want to look at one traditional provider, so they include the iShares ESG Aware MSCI EM ETF on their list as well.

Dan and Sharon's Shortlist

iShares ESG Aware MSCI EM ETF

Amana Developing World Fund

Calvert Emerging Markets Equity Fund

Domini International Opportunities Fund

Dan and Sharon's priority was engagement, so the first thing they did was look for evidence of their fund provider's engagement. In the process, they learned a couple of interesting things:

- For their BlackRock fund, they found that BlackRock's voting policies weren't particularly stringent and that the company appeared to be trying to cater both to sustainable and traditional investors at the same time with their engagement efforts.

- For the Amana fund, they learned that the fund was actually run by Saturna Capital. But more interestingly, the fund was run according to "Islamic Principles." This wasn't what they had expected, but they were interested to learn more.

- The Calvert fund held a lot of companies that Dan and Sharon had heard of, and they were impressed with the detailed engagement reporting that Calvert did and their active leadership in the sustainable investing field. However, they need to pay a fee to access the fund on their Schwab platform.

- The Domini fund went above and beyond to detail their engagement with companies, reporting quarterly on their efforts to do so. And their proxy voting guidelines were by far the most stringent of any of the four they looked at. But this fund was very young compared to the others from sustainable-only providers, and its financial performance lagged the others as well.

Dan and Sharon agreed that the BlackRock fund was not a great option as it was lacking the engagement that they were looking for, despite its low fees. They were willing to pay the fees for a provider that was going to fight for their values.

They also agreed that the Calvert fund, while fitting a lot of what they wanted, was not worth paying the extra charges required by Schwab to invest in them. They preferred the engagement from Domini, and the Amana fund had performed better over the last few years.

The choice came down to the Domini International Opportunities Fund and the Amana Developing World Fund. After looking closer at both organizations, Dan and Sharon decided to go with the Domini fund. While it had worse performance and a shorter track record, Domini as a company had an extensive track record and set itself apart with its engagement practices. Dan and Sharon moved their money within Schwab to the Domini fund.

In Short...

Choosing investments for your money is a decision with a lot of con-sequences, and being a sustainable investor adds a layer to an already challenging process. In our view, the key to making a start as a sustainable investor is to find an easy way to take a step. You don't need to make a forever decision or try to make the perfect choice. These tools and this framework are enough to make a good decision—a foundation for all the impact you will have in years to come.

Of course, there is an alternative to working through this exercise yourself—you could talk with an advisor or financial planner. If you do, there are a few things we think you should know.

CHAPTER 9

Do I Need an Advisor to Invest Sustainably?

Here's an interesting set of data points from a 2021 report by Cerulli Associates, which surveyed both financial advisors and individual investors about sustainable investing.

- More than half (58 percent) of surveyed advisors said "[a] lack of investor demand was a significant factor" preventing their adoption of ESG strategies. "Advisors maintain a widely held belief that demand for ESG strategies among their clients is a non-issue."
- At the very same time, Cerulli's survey of U.S. retail investor households found that nearly half (44 percent) of households would prefer to invest in an environmental or socially responsible way—far more than the "handful" of clients that advisors report proactively reaching out around the topic.

All the way back in the introduction of this book we discussed the "circle of change"—how you, as an individual investor, can create an industry that is more responsive to your interests by asking the right questions and pushing the right people. A more responsive industry is one that provides you with better products and works to give better answers to the questions you ask.

Nowhere is your influence more tangible than in discussions with financial advisors. Simply making a call, telling them what you're looking for, and walking away if they're not ready to provide it to you is a powerful move as a sustainable investor. If advisors aren't hearing from people like you, then maybe they should!

We're going to spend some time in this chapter talking about what an advisor could do for you. But at the same time, ask yourself this—what can you be doing for your financial advisor?

The Roles a Financial Advisor (FA) Can Play for a Sustainable Investor

Do you need a financial advisor to be a successful sustainable investor?

No, you don't necessarily *need* one. You can do the research on your own and make appropriate investment decisions. If you are young and just starting out, your investment portfolio is likely to be pretty simple. Until you amass, say, more than $100,000, having an advisor is not going to be terribly cost-effective. Even if you have substantial savings, DIY investing may still appeal to you. It gives you a lot of control, and it forces you to think deeply through challenging financial issues.

And yet at a certain point, there's good reason to consider getting a financial advisor.

Financial advisors can serve an important role for certain investors. Investments are just one part of your personal financial ecosystem, and it helps to have someone looking at the big picture. Decisions you make today will have consequences far down the road—not just regarding the financial resources you acquire, but also in terms of taxation, family preparedness, philanthropy, and beyond.

That's true for every investor. But sustainable investors can benefit from an added level of support. You're not just trying to understand the financial aspects of your investments; you're trying to understand the impact of the companies you invest in, and how those fit your personal values. You may be looking to take advantage of proxy votes where possible to directly vote your values—or at the very least to invest with funds that are likely to do that for you.

This becomes even more true as you reach the higher rungs on the Ladder of Impact, where your portfolio is larger and your financial situation more complex. Advisors can provide a window into private investment opportunities with more direct positive impacts. They can develop strategies that tie into your philanthropic pursuits and may be able to connect you with other sustainability-minded financial experts in your local community.

A financial advisor that is committed to helping you invest your values can help you do all of that. And, they can help you stay on top of investing information that may be important to you—a critical job in an industry that is rapidly evolving.

Finding the Right Advisor Matters—A Lot

Here's the trouble—not all financial advisors are great stewards for sustainable investors. Some of them don't like the idea of sustainable investing. Some of them don't want or need to change with the times. A lot of them don't have the time to do extra research. Many will dismiss sustainable investing as a bad investment, a passing trend, something that doesn't "work," a distraction from more important goals. Many of them, as noted in the introduction to this chapter, simply don't think that their clients want to invest sustainably.

We know—we've talked to a lot of these advisors. Those conversations aren't always great!

But there are also numerous firms that specialize in providing advice to sustainable investors. And there are advisor directories that let you search for advisors with a sustainable focus, including ones by US SIF, Certified Financial Planner Board of Standards, and Onyx Advisors. Financial advisors can get ESG certifications from organizations like the College for Financial Planning or the CFA Institute.

You have to search for them, but there are advisors out there who are willing to learn something new, listen to what you're looking for, and partner with you to help you get where you'd like to go.

We know—we've talked to a lot of these advisors, too. And those conversations can be great.

Sustainability-focused advisors want you to know that you don't have to do it yourself or be stuck with automated robo-advisors. You can get real human advice from advisors that keep costs down by charging hourly or by project. Some use subscription models to spread costs out over time. There are many low-fee, no-minimum ways to invest in line with your values.

How to Start a Sustainability Conversation With an Advisor

Whether you are just starting to look for an advisor, or you want to start discussing values with the advisor you already have, the best way to ensure that your values are part of the conversation is to bring them up yourself. For example:

- Engage them in a broader conversation about values. This is probably a question they should be asking you! But if they haven't, be the one to bring it up. Ask them about their values—what drives them, other than money? Tell them about your views and expectations.
- Discuss their experience. Ask the advisor about their history supporting sustainable investors and some examples of investments they have recommended.
- Get their help investigating a sustainable investment. Share with them the name of a fund or stock that interests you and ask them to determine if it's a suitable investment for you given your financial situation and priorities.
- Talk about proxy voting. Ask them to show you the proxy voting guidelines of any fund company they recommend to you. Remember: you have the right to vote by proxy on matters pertaining to the governance of the companies you invest in. Most asset managers do this voting for you, but they document the guidelines they use to vote proxies on your behalf. It is your right to know those guidelines, and it's a good idea to talk them over with your advisor.

Of course, you don't need to choose or stay with an advisor if you don't like the answers to these questions. But if you do stay with your advisor, bear in mind that you don't need to ask these questions just once. You can help your advisor be more proactive and open to change by continuing to explain your interest and asking tough questions.

In Short...

At the end of the day, the "right" advisor for you is going to be one that listens to your concerns that can supplement your knowledge base with their own strengths and can be a partner for you as much as a provider.

It may be that you don't need an advisor, but if you think you do, these conversations are valuable—to you and to your advisor. A successful relationship with an advisor is built on trust. And trust is built on strong communication.

CHAPTER 10

Amp Your Impact With Action

It's probably obvious by now, but: we believe that sustainable investing is one of the most potent acts of change you can engage in. The world is full of change agents and power brokers who want to remake the world in their own image. But sustainable investing is different—it's a grassroots idea borne out of the soil of your beliefs, your neighbors, and your community. It provides a voice to everyone who invests.

But even we can acknowledge that investing doesn't always *feel* that powerful, on its own. Investing is a long-term, "slow and steady wins the race," kind of thing. It doesn't always have that satisfying punch.

Luckily, there's a fix for that. You can amp up the impact you have as a sustainable investor by taking simple actions. In some cases, you can quite dramatically expand the reach of sustainable investing and make the entire industry better with just a Google search or a phone call.

Taking action is a great way to feel like you are truly making a difference. But to be honest, we have a secondary motive for wanting to encourage action—because sustainable investing as an industry is evolving at a very fast pace. What's possible today, the options in front of you right now—well, they all might look quite different a year from now.

In fact, we hope they do look different. We'd like to see more options and better reporting. We want better tools to help you compare sustainable funds. Sustainable investing has come a long way in the last 40 years. It has a ways to go.

And you have a hand in this. You can create a better world for sustainable investors like yourself by being vocal and engaged. The more sustainable investors make themselves heard, the more that the investment industry will move toward solutions that satisfy your needs.

Here are a couple of places where you can apply pressure in a meaningful way this year.

Make Your Presence Felt

The influence you can exert as a values investor goes well beyond the money you have to invest. Even if your investments are small, as a stockholder, or a shareholder in a fund, you are a legal owner and you have a voice. Learning how to use that voice is an important part of maximizing your impact.

For example, fund companies pay close attention to how their customers and potential customers interact with them. Every time you download an impact report, click on a sustainable fund, or search "ESG" on their website, that's another data point that shows them that there is demand for sustainable products.

And you can go farther. If you have a question, call the provider up and ask. For example, you might want to know:

- How does this sustainable fund work?
- What other products do you offer for sustainable investors?
- How can you be sure greenwashing isn't going on?

Even if you don't get a satisfying answer, just the fact that you asked the question will be noted. When enough people ask the same questions, it will affect their decisions about what kind of products to create and what kind of information they need to provide.

We have already seen this process play out among large-scale institutional investors. About a decade ago, pension funds, nonprofits, and endowments, for example, started asking their investment providers these exact questions. As better sustainability information became available in the marketplace, it started to make little sense for institutions to invest in ways that undermine their missions. Why would a union pension fund invest in companies with poor labor relations records?

Fund companies can be slow to change, but when big money asks tough questions, the pace of change speeds up. You may not think that your personal investments qualify as "big money," but when they are a part of a $500 million sustainable fund, your voice begins to matter.

Most major companies produce materials that answer these kinds of questions, but if no one asks for them, the materials will wither down to nothing over time. Even if you have no intention of reading the fund company's literature, ask for it anyway.

Ask for an Impact Report

Another action you can take: If you're not already receiving them, ask your fund provider to send you their impact report. Not all providers create them, but if you consistently request them, you're sending an important signal that you're paying attention to their sustainability strategy.

Impact reports vary widely, and some are far more helpful than others. But they generally provide additional detail about the sustainable strategy you are investing in—the kind of strategy that is being used, the kind of data they are looking at, and the kind of impacts they believe they have achieved.

When you receive an impact report, flip through it, and ask yourself—does this report seem authentic and believable? Does it give you answers to questions that are important to you? If not, you can always call your provider and tell them so.

Check Into Your Workplace Retirement Plan

If your 401(k) or 403(b) retirement plan doesn't have a sustainable option in it, don't give up! You can look for opportunities to expand the menu of sustainable options available to you and your fellow employees. For example:

- *Know your plan administrator.* Retirement plans need to have someone in charge of day-to-day administrative tasks. Depending on the size and structure of your company, that plan administrator may be the owner, a member of your human resources department, a designated employee, or even an outsourced company. Whoever they are, find out their name and contact information. Ask your boss, your HR department, or look at your plan documents.

- *Ask your plan administrator about sustainable options in your plan.* You may already know what is available in your plan, but it's still good to ask. Asking registers your interest in having sustainable options. If there are no sustainable options, ask why. This will give you insight into whether there is a specific impediment or just a general lack of familiarity.
- *Ask your plan administrator what it would take to include sustainable options in your plan.* Plan administrators can't make decisions about investment options, but they should know who does make those decisions and what the process is.
- *Ask your fellow employees if they have an interest in sustainable options.* If you can demonstrate a broad interest in including sustainable options in your plan, your odds of getting them go up. Take a list of signatures to your plan administrator and ask for their help in sharing that information with decision makers.
- *Share US SIF resources.* US SIF (the Forum for Sustainable and Responsible Investment) is a trade group and research organization that offers general research and specific guides for making sustainable investments. If you're feeling that the plan administrator or company leadership needs to bone up on the case for sustainable investing, US SIF's tools are an excellent resource.

Tell Others in Your Community(ies)

People don't always like to talk about their investments, but based on our experiences, there is a powerful hunger for ways to invest sustainably. People are attracted to the idea immediately; they just aren't sure how to go about it. Sharing your experiences—of defining your values, of looking for options to fit those values, and of taking action—is a powerful force for positive change.

You don't have to limit those conversations to friends and family. You can engage with organizations you are a part of that would be interested in sustainable investing if they knew enough about it. Many organizations would be good candidates for sustainable investing, including as follows.

Charities and volunteer organizations. Large foundations, endowments, and national nonprofits were early adopters of sustainable investing. But the *average* charity or volunteer organization may not know anything about it. If you donate to a nonprofit like this, ask them: "do you invest in a way that supports your mission?" Ask them to show you the receipts. This is exactly how those large foundations, endowments, and national nonprofits came to adopt sustainable investing in the first place.

Churches and religious groups. If you're an active member of your religious community, start a conversation about sustainable investing. You can talk with leaders about their approach to investing, and you can talk to fellow congregants about the opportunity to invest in alignment with their values. Of course, people will have different priorities and fighting styles, but everyone can benefit from knowing these options exist.

Groups that like to get involved. Maybe you've joined an environmentally focused group or a local co-op. Maybe you participate in marches and meetings around women's rights or social justice. Any group that wants to have an impact can make more of a difference by engaging in or promoting sustainable investing.

Your experiences make you a powerful ambassador for sustainable investing. And now you know that you have a partner in these efforts—Till Investors. We want to hear your stories, so please—come to our website and tell us what you've experienced. Or ask us a question. We want to help.

Stare Down Your Advisor (If You Have One)

We talked earlier about how to discuss sustainable investing with an advisor, if you use one or are considering hiring one. We also mentioned that many advisors have been slow to embrace values investing, since it's something they may not be that familiar with. Don't be dismayed or dissuaded if they put you off. Keep asking for information about sustainable options and ask them to look for more information on your investments, like impact reports or proxy voting guidelines. You can share some of the resources we've mentioned in this book and ask them to come up with a plan for incorporating your values. You're hiring them to help you, but they might need your leadership on this issue.

Finally: Share and Stay Aware

Sustainable investing is very much on the front line of change in today's America. It's fascinating for us to see who's making real advances, who's debating what, and who's clinging for dear life to old, unsustainable ways of doing things. We talk to investment people, go to conferences, and talk with investors to figure out the story of investing for impact as it grows and changes:

- Which companies really are changing the world with better products or practices?
- Are fund companies getting any better at creating—and sharing information about—sustainable funds?
- Which proxy votes are upending established businesses?
- What are regulators doing to eliminate greenwashing?
- How are the opponents of sustainable investing fighting back and what can we do about it?
- What are other sustainability advocates doing?

But you don't have to keep an eye on changes, improvements, or opportunities in sustainable investing, because we already do that and share what we find. Just follow us on social media, and you can keep up with it too. If what you see piques your interest, share it with friends. Our goal is to support you—today, tomorrow, and for the life of your sustainable investing journey.

In Short...

You've got what it takes to be a sustainable investor. Go do it! And as you go, keep the following in mind.

Sustainable investing is already bringing real change to the world. It has the potential for so much more. But it's only going to go as far as sustainable investors like you are willing to push it. Your money is your vote. Your actions are your influence. Save the planet. Save for retirement. Save for yourself and for your community all at once. Spread the word, raise awareness, and break the silence. Sustainable investing tomorrow can be even better than it is today. You can help make it happen!

APPENDIX

Fund Manager Profiles

Sustainable investors have many hundreds of options to choose from. Honestly, it's a lot. But you can narrow down your options significantly by knowing a little something about the types of companies that offer sustainable funds.

We want to make this easier for you, so in this appendix, we're sharing several of our Fund Manager Profiles. It includes several well-known names in the sustainable universe, drawn from a list of the largest sustainable mutual funds and ETFs, and it is current as of April 2023. We're also including some summary information about other relatively well-known providers of sustainable funds.

This list is not comprehensive, and we are not endorsing these options as a fit for your specific interests. We're just trying to help you get the ball rolling. It is our view that these fund companies and their products are worth your time and effort to research.

Till Investors will also be including Fund Manager Profiles on the tillinvestors.com website. It is our plan to update and expand the number of profiles over time. As a book purchaser, you can get a free copy of the latest version of our Fund Manager Profiles using the code ESG4ME.

Sustainable-Only Providers to Know

The sustainable-only fund providers are the innovators and the advocates. They only offer sustainable strategies and are often out front in considering how investor values can be evaluated alongside financial considerations. They are also typically leaders in company engagement, demanding better company data and proposing changes in the way companies do business.

Parnassus

www.parnassus.com

Who Are They?

Parnassus is an established leader in sustainable investing, having been in business since 1984. They take a mainstream approach, applying a sustainability lens to general equity and fixed-income funds.

What Do They Offer?

Parnassus opts for quality over quantity, offering a handful of broad equity funds and one fixed-income fund. Their flagship offering is their "Core Equity Fund," which they describe as a "large blend fund" made up of 40 stocks. The fund is the largest actively managed mutual fund in the United States with a sustainability focus.

Do They Say What They Do?

In general terms, yes. They provide an extensive discussion about their approach to ESG data and a short summary of their proxy voting policies, and a couple of case studies. When you dig into their fund literature, they talk broadly about responsible investment and are open about the challenges in deciding which companies make the cut. They are very clear that they are investors first, and sustainability is baked into their investment process.

Do They Do What They Say?

It's not always easy to tell. Some things are clear: They divest from oil and gas, which is easy enough to verify. They report all of their proxy votes. But there isn't a lot of information about how they apply their Sustainable Investment principles in their investment process. You may read an entire quarterly commentary without an ESG issue being raised. This may be by design—they may only bring up sustainability issues when they are primary drivers of a decision—but we would prefer to see more detail. Parnassus leans on their reputation and history of investing sustainably.

Who Is This Good for?

People who want to take a measured approach to sustainable investing. Those who want to invest in strong performing companies, but only if they are good corporate citizens.

Fund to Know: Parnassus Core Equity Fund—Investor Shares				
Actively Managed Large Blend Fund made up of around 40 U.S. and International Stocks with an eye on ESG considerations				
Inception date	Assets (Millions)	Minimum investment	Expense ratio—Net	Expense ratio—Gross
08/31/1992	$26,956.40	$2,500.00	0.82%	0.82%

Calvert

www.calvert.com

Who Are They?

Calvert was founded in 1976 and in many ways, it was the company that put socially responsible investing on the map. Company ownership has changed multiple times but the firm's commitment to being a sustainability leader has not wavered. They have significant in-house research resources and one of the more evolved sustainable investing lineups in the marketplace.

What Do They Offer?

Calvert offers over 20 actively managed funds, including core equity funds, funds with a specific ESG theme, and an unusually wide range of bond funds. Their largest fund is the actively managed Calvert Equity Fund. They also offer a few passive index funds, the largest of which is the Calvert US Large-Cap Core Responsible Index Fund. In early 2023, they launched a series of ETFs featuring some of the lowest fees of any specialty ESG fund manager available.

Do They Say What They Do?

Calvert has a lot to say about their investment process. They invest according to their publicly available "Principles for Responsible Investment," and go into great detail on their website about how they incorporate those principles into their investments. They release a very detailed look at their proxy voting policies and explain how they engage with companies and the wider investment industry on sustainability issues.

Do They Do What They Say?

There is strong evidence that they do. You will see references to ESG themes in their quarterly commentaries, and they even release an "Impact

Metric" report for their Calvert Equity Fund. They make their proxy votes public as well. Beyond that, they are very active in the Sustainable Investment community, being early, active participants with groups like the U.S. Sustainable Investment Forum and the UN's Principles for Responsible Investment.

Who Is This Good for?

People who want to align themselves with a proactive leader, even if it has meant slightly higher fees and slightly lower returns in the past. (To be fair, a recent change in management has improved the funds' fee structures.)

Fund to Know: Calvert Equity Fund—Class A				
Actively managed Large Growth Fund with a framework based on Calvert's Principles for Responsible Investment.				
Inception date	Assets (Millions)	Minimum investment	Expense ratio—Net	Expense ratio—Gross
08/24/1987	$5,855.92	$2,500.00	0.91%	0.91%

Fund to Know: Calvert U.S. Large Cap Core Responsible Index Fund—Class A				
Passive fund that filters out U.S. companies that don't meet Calvert's Principles for Responsible Investment. The fund holds about 800 companies out of a pool of 1000.				
Inception date	Assets (Millions)	Minimum investment	Expense ratio—Net	Expense ratio—Gross
06/30/2000	$4,116.97	$5,000.00	0.49%	0.59%

IMPAX

www.impaxam.com

Who Are They?

Impax Asset Management is a British company that was an early proponent of creating sustainable investing strategies. In the United States, Impax owns the Impax Funds series of sustainable mutual funds. Impax remains a relatively small company but they have several funds that are popular and respected.

What Do They Offer?

Impax offers 11 funds with sustainability strategies. While they offer a few broad-based equity and bond options, their most popular products include their thematic funds, such as Impax Ellevate Global Women's Leadership Fund. In 2021, they renamed and repositioned a number of their funds to give them more specific sustainable investment mandates.

Do They Say What They Do?

It depends on which funds you are looking at. Their thematic funds provide a lot of documentation detailing how they are constructed. Meanwhile, their broader-based funds rely on a proprietary "Impax Sustainability Lens." We are often dubious about proprietary strategies, but to be fair, the company goes into great detail explaining its approach to ESG elsewhere on its website. Impax also posts their proxy voting guidelines, which are very specific particularly as it relates to board construction.

Do They Do What They Say?

Disappointingly, the commentaries for the broader funds don't talk much about sustainability. That means investors are putting some faith in Impax itself, which is reasonable given their track record and history. For the thematic funds, it is clear they are doing what they say, in their holdings, and in their commentaries. They talk about why they hold the companies that they do and what that means for the fund's performance. They report their proxy votes as well.

Who Is This Good for?

Impax offers several good options, but their fees on some funds are relatively high. People who identify with the thematic funds offered by Impax are most likely to be happy with their investment.

Fund to Know: Impax Global Environmental Markets Fund				
Active fund that identifies companies that provide environmental solutions including net carbon reductions and resource efficiency.				
Inception date	Assets (Millions)	Minimum investment	Expense ratio—Net	Expense ratio—Gross
3/27/2008	$2,135.51	$1,000	1.15%	1.15%

Fund to Know: Impax Ellevate Global Women's Leadership Fund				
Passive fund that tracks an in-house index that has a formula to identify companies with strong numbers of female leaders.				
Inception date	Assets (Millions)	Minimum investment	Expense ratio—Net	Expense ratio—Gross
6/4/2014*	$780.68	$1,000	0.76%	0.76%

*The fund has actually been in existence since October 1993 but underwent a reorganization and changed its methodology in 2014.

Domini Funds
www.domini.com

Who Are They?

Domini was founded in the 1990s by Amy Domini, a well-known advocate for investing with impact. While Domini invests with financial results in mind, they are highly attuned to the objective of driving change and are more aggressive about engaging the companies they invest in than their average competitor.

What Do They Offer?

Domini's focus is on impact, and therefore they keep their investment options simple. They only offer five funds, the two largest of which are a U.S.-focused equity fund and a non-U.S. equity fund. They also offer a bond fund, a sustainable solutions fund, and an international opportunities fund.

Do They Say What They Do?

Unapologetically yes. Domini hangs their hat on the impact that they create. They are very specific about how they invest, and even more specific about how they engage with companies and how they vote for company proxies. All of their funds divest from what they deem to be bad actors. Of all of the fund managers that we have reviewed in this book, Domini commits the most effort to describe what they do and how.

Do They Do What They Say?

Again, overwhelmingly yes. They create extensive quarterly and annual impact reports, report on their engagements, and detail their proxy votes. Their fund commentaries speak specifically to their investment strategies and how those strategies affected performance. Whenever there is a public discussion about a sustainability issue, they are on the front lines or close to it. They pride themselves on making their actions public and telling their story.

Who Is This Good for?

People who want to align themselves with an activist investor, who want to know exactly what their money is doing in the world, even if it means paying higher fees and possibly earning lower short-term returns relative to other funds.

Fund to Know: Domini Impact Equity Fund				
Active fund that has both "core" and "thematic" themes, focused on US-based mid-to-large companies with strong ESG profiles.				
Inception date	Assets (Millions)	Minimum investment	Expense ratio—Net	Expense ratio—Gross
12/1/2018*	$916.87	$2,500	1.09%	1.09%

*This fund has been active since 1991, but underwent a strategy change in 2018.

Other Large Sustainable-Only Providers
With Long Histories

Trillium Asset Management

www.trilliuminvest.com

Trillium was founded by Joan Bavaria, a committed socially responsible investing advocate who also cofounded US SIF in 1984. The company has a highly evolved sustainability strategy and offers a range of core equity and bond products. However, most of them are only available to institutional or high-net-worth investors. The company does offer two mutual funds to the general public and also acts as a subadvisor for the John Hancock ESG Large-Cap Core Fund and the Green Century Balanced Fund.

Saturna Capital/Amana Mutual Funds

www.saturna.com/amana

Saturna is an umbrella company that offers sustainable funds as well as the Sextant series, which does not have a defined sustainable mandate. However, they are best known for the Amana funds, which are invested according to Islamic principles. Broadly, that means the funds take a conservative approach, avoiding interest as well as investments in liquor, pornography, gambling, and banks.

Green Century Funds

www.greencentury.com

Remember Ralph Nader? He and his partner Donald Ross created "Public Interest Research Groups" (PIRGs) in the 1970s to lobby for social interests. Those PIRGs still exist, and in the early 1990s, several PIRGs got together to found Green Century. Green Century only offers three mutual funds, two of which are index funds, and one of which is managed by Trillium. However, they are unique in that the company itself is a nonprofit. All profits are returned to the PIRGs, who use them to fund environmental and public health campaigns.

The Big Names (and Their Sustainable Offerings)

Everybody knows the big guns in the investment world—their names are plastered in advertisements everywhere you go. These are the stalwarts who have long histories of success in meeting the needs of investors. Many of them are only recently adapting to investor demand for sustainable product offerings, but they are bringing talent, experience, and major resources to the table.

BlackRock
www.blackrock.com

Who Are They?

BlackRock is the world's largest asset manager, with a primary focus on low-cost, passively managed exchange-traded funds (ETFs). In recent years, CEO Larry Fink has become an influential advocate for ESG investment strategies. However, it should be noted that only a small portion of BlackRock's overall assets under management are invested in alignment with ESG principles.

What Do They Offer?

A whole lot. Their biggest sustainable funds—which are some of the largest sustainable funds in the world—are passive ETFs under their "iShares" label. Their funds track custom indexes of sustainable companies in various categories, as defined by a third party (MSCI). They also offer thematic passive funds like a Clean Energy ETF and a Green Bond fund. On the active side, they offer numerous funds with sustainability labels, and in 2020 they launched a suite of "Impact" funds.

Do They Say What They Do?

For their passive ETFs, it is easier to see the methodology and, particularly with the MSCI funds, there is good documentation of how the indexes are constructed. The active funds are more of a mixed bag. There is a lot of "in BlackRock's view" language, a lot of "may include" language, and a lot of "as determined by BlackRock's proprietary research." This is tough to lean on because BlackRock's opinions on ESG and sustainable investing can shift from year to year. They also extensively discuss their proxy voting guidelines but give themselves a lot of latitude within those guidelines.

Do They Do What They Say?

For the passive ETFs, yes. Their strategies are clear and easy to confirm. For the active funds, again, it's harder to say. With not much insight into the process, it's hard to trust that the results reflect that process. The other big challenge is that when it comes to proxy voting, BlackRock is trying to appeal to people with values that might be pro- or anti-sustainability. As such, they don't always vote with sustainability in mind. Even with that, they have ended up in the crosshairs of conservatives looking to pick a fight with ESG fund providers.

Who Is This Good for?

BlackRock's sustainable ETFs are popular because they are very inexpensive and relatively straightforward. They are a good way to dip a toe into sustainable investing and to do it with a company that has vast influence in the investment world—even if that impact isn't always what you would like.

Fund to Know: iShares ESG Aware MSCI USA ETF				
Passive fund that tracks an index created by MSCI that identifies companies with positive ESG characteristics. Holds around 300 companies.				
Inception date	Assets (Millions)	Minimum investment	Expense ratio—Net	Expense ratio—Gross
12/1/2016	$22,376.69	<$100	0.15%	0.15%

Fund to Know: iShares Global Clean Energy ETF				
Passive fund that tracks the S&P Global Clean Energy index, which holds around 100 companies involved in the production of clean energy.				
Inception date	Assets (Millions)	Minimum investment	Expense ratio—Net	Expense ratio—Gross
6/24/2008	$5,628.01	<$100	0.42%	0.42%

Vanguard

www.vanguard.com

Who Are They?

Vanguard has been around in one fashion or another since 1929, and they have long been viewed as an advocate for shareholder interests. They were a pioneer in popularizing index investing as a cheaper, more accessible alternative to expensive investment products. But they have been a little slow to adopt sustainable investing strategies.

What Do They Offer?

Vanguard does have a handful of products labeled "ESG." Not surprisingly, their largest funds are passive ETFs—both focused on stocks, one an international fund and one U.S.-only, both of which deploy a simple "avoiding" style. But they also offer two actively managed ESG funds, which are managed by subadvisors. Their brokerage customers can access their fund platform, which makes it possible to invest in non-Vanguard ESG fund providers within your account. Most of their sustainable offerings are less than five years old.

Do They Say What They Do?

Mostly. Their passive ETFs simply divest from bad actors, and they get very specific about who those bad actors are and how they are identified. The actively managed funds rely on communications from the subadvisors, but both go into good detail about their investment processes.

Do They Do What They Say?

Again, with the passive ETFs, it's very easy to verify their divestment efforts. Vanguard does vote company proxies on behalf of fund shareholders, but it's not entirely clear how they determine their positions. For their actively managed funds, proxy voting and engagement are done by the subadvisors, and both are clear about how they do so.

Who Is This Good for?

Vanguard funds pride themselves on being among the cheapest available investment options. People whose fighting style is divesting may be comfortable with their ETFs. They are also an easy choice for existing Vanguard customers who are looking for a more sustainable approach.

Fund to Know: Vanguard ESG U.S. Stock ETF				
Passive fund that tracks an index that divests from oil and gas, weapons, alcohol, tobacco, and more.				
Inception date	Assets (Millions)	Minimum investment	Expense ratio—Net	Expense ratio—Gross
09/18/2018	$6,800	<$100	0.09%	0.09%

Fund to Know: Vanguard Global ESG Select Stock Fund				
Actively managed fund that invests in 35–45 mid-large sized companies with leading ESG practices and strong finances.				
Inception date	Assets (Millions)	Minimum investment	Expense ratio—Net	Expense ratio—Gross
06/05/2019	$773.9	$3,000	0.56%	0.56%

Fidelity

www.fidelity.com

Who Are They?

Fidelity is another global investment giant. Fidelity offers a very wide range of quality funds at a reasonable price, but they are also well known for their state-of-the-art services. For example, Fidelity brokerage customers can access a highly effective and detailed online tool for screening and selecting specific funds, either from Fidelity or many other providers.

What Do They Offer?

Fidelity offers a lot of options for sustainable investors. For example, they offer a low-cost Sustainability Index Fund that is managed by a subadvisor and tracks the MSCI ESG Index. They also offer some actively managed thematic funds like a Women's Leadership Fund and a Water Sustainability Fund. All of their sustainable funds, however, are very young—mostly under five years old. For brokerage customers, Fidelity's fund platform offers easy access to BlackRock's iShares ETFs and many other sustainable fund providers, including Parnassus, Calvert, Impax, and others.

Do They Say What They Do?

At a high level, yes. For each of their in-house funds, they provide a monthly fact sheet that gives a good summary of the investment approach. But often the prospectuses for the funds are relatively low in detail compared to their competitors. Their proxy vote guidelines are very broad and make no real commitment to issues like diversity or environmental policies.

Do They Do What They Say?

Largely yes. Their monthly fact sheets show holdings that line up with their strategies. The most informative language they release is in the form of Portfolio Manager Q&As for their thematic funds, which give significant insight into the manager's thought process and how they consider the theme of the fund alongside financial factors. Where Fidelity comes up short is reporting proxy votes. They do say that their ESG fund managers can vote differently from Fidelity as a whole, but they don't make it easy to see what those votes are.

Who Is This Good for?

People who want easy access to a broad set of fund providers. Fidelity's platform is the best we have come across for choosing between both in-house and outside funds, allowing you to invest in specialty providers while using Fidelity's superior user interface. Their thematic funds are young but well-documented.

Fidelity U.S. Sustainability Index Fund				
Passive fund that tracks an ESG Index comprised of strong ESG performers amongst large/medium businesses in the United States, provided by MSCI.				
Inception date	Assets (Millions)	Minimum investment	Expense ratio—Net	Expense ratio—Gross
05/09/2017	$2,258.06	<$100	0.11%	0.11%

Fidelity Environment and Alternative Energy Fund				
Actively managed fund that invests in businesses involved in renewable or alternative energy or related technologies.				
Inception date	Assets (Millions)	Minimum investment	Expense ratio—Net	Expense ratio—Gross
07/01/2010*	$671.12	<$100	0.79%	0.79%

*This fund has existed since 1989 but underwent a strategy change in 2010. The fund also underwent a name change in 2021 but kept its same strategy.

Other Large Asset Managers With Sustainable Offerings

Invesco

www.invesco.com

Invesco is a long-established mutual fund company that in recent years has jumped deeply into the sustainable ETF market. They offer seven ETFs with at least a five-year track record, and a range of interesting thematic funds, such as the Invesco MSCI Green Building ETF and the Invesco WilderHill Green Energy ETF.

Putnam Investments

www.putnam.com

Offers a handful of sustainable funds with a track record back to the early 90s. Their largest sustainable fund is their "Sustainable Leaders" fund, one of the largest in the world, with performance similar to Parnassus funds, albeit with higher expenses.

PIMCO

www.pimco.com

PIMCO is primarily known for its fixed-income expertise. PIMCO's lineup includes ESG-oriented bond funds, such as the PIMCO Climate Bond Fund, and a bond ESG ETF. Sustainable bond strategies are early in their development and can be hard for income-oriented investors to find, so it's comforting to see the experts at PIMCO at the helm. On the other hand, PIMCO's ESG bond funds are fairly new, and it's not that clear what their strategy is or what the risk and return profile of the funds is likely to be.

TIAA/Nuveen

www.nuveen.com

TIAA is a name familiar to many teachers, government employees, university staff, and nonprofit organizations, as TIAA-CREF has been a go-to organization for their pension and retirement funds. TIAA-CREF's parent organization, TIAA, merged with Nuveen in 2017, a bond-focused asset management firm. Since then, TIAA has expanded their sustainable offerings, which now include a series of TIAA-CREF mutual funds and more than a dozen Nuveen ETFs.

Thematic Funds

Sustainable-only fund providers and big-name players often have thematic funds in their lineup that are worth investigating. But if you want to find investments that hit hard on the values you care about, the place to look is ETFs.

Sustainable ETFs are a relatively recent development—few have more than a five-year history of performance. Still, some of them are quite popular. Here is an overview of thematic ETFs that have attracted a significant amount of attention and/or investment.

Gender Focus

SPDR SSGA Gender Diversity Index ETF (ticker: SHE). This ETF from State Street Global Advisors screens for companies that have greater gender diversity on their boards or in their senior leadership ranks, relative to other firms in the same sector. This ETF dates to 2016 and is considered the first of its kind.

Impact Shares YWCA Women's Empowerment ETF (ticker: WOMN). Impact Shares is a nonprofit that partners with other organizations to translate their social missions into investable portfolios. In this case, they have partnered with the YWCA to create an ETF that invests in the Morningstar Women's Empowerment Index. They then donate any net profits from the portfolio back to the YWCA.

Clean Energy Focus

First Trust NASDAQ Clean Edge Green Energy Index Fund (ticker: QCLN). Focuses on emerging clean-energy technologies, such as solar photovoltaics, wind power, advanced batteries, fuel cells, and electric vehicles.

ALPS Clean Energy ETF (ticker: ACES). Invests in renewables and "clean energy" technologies, meaning the products and services that enable the evolution of a more sustainable energy sector.

Etho Climate Leadership U.S. ETF (ticker: ETHO). Etho claims that the companies held in this ETF have a combined climate footprint of over 80 percent better than the S&P 500. It avoids fossil-fuel companies, invests in new climate technologies, and seeks out climate leaders across all industries.

Other

Adasina Social Justice All Cap Global ETF (ticker: JSTC). Adasina was started by Rachel Robasciotti, a successful investment advisor and committed advocate for social justice. Their ETF is just one branch of a broad approach to using financial capital to bring positive change to women, minorities, and other disadvantaged populations.

U.S. Vegan Climate ETF (ticker: VEGN). This unusual ETF appeals to those who are driven by both animal rights concerns and the impact of climate destruction. While the connection between the two themes is tenuous, it has proven relatively popular.

Ecofin Global Water ESG Fund (ticker: EBLU). Water is a popular investment theme among fund and ETF providers, in part because it's a relatively easy-to-execute investment. Rather than evaluating companies on their behaviors, water funds simply provide a source of funding for companies likely to benefit from large water-access projects.

NewDay Ocean Health (ticker: AHOY). NewDay is a relatively small player with a relatively small ETF, but it demonstrates how specifically you can use ETFs to target issues that are of concern to you. Bear in mind though—as with most thematic funds, the theme may drive investment decisions more than performance does.

Impact Shares NAACP Minority Empowerment ETF (ticker: NACP). As described above, Impact Shares is a nonprofit that donates any net proceeds from their funds back to their nonprofit partners—in this case, the NAACP. The fund tracks the performance of the Morningstar Minority Empowerment Index.

About the Authors

Kylelane Purcell

Co-Founder, Till Investors

Kyle believes that understanding money is important, valuable, and even exciting. After all, how many things are more interesting than your money, and the things you can do with it? That's why she's such a proponent of teaching the everyday investor the ins and outs of the game.

Kyle has held communications leadership roles at several financial companies, including Morningstar, American Century, and T. Rowe Price. But in 2005, in search of a better life balance while raising three young boys, she started Purcell Communications as a financial writing and education firm. Over time, PurcellCom grew into one of the largest and most sustainable companies of its kind.

PurcellCom also developed a unique expertise in writing about socially responsible investing, or ESG investing, having worked with several pioneering firms in the field. Kyle's knowledge of sustainable investing found its match in current Till co-founder Ben Vivari. Combining her analytical aptitude with his expertise in sustainable business, they've made Till the premier resource for those with a desire to invest sustainably.

Ben Vivari, CSRIC®

Co-Founder, Till Investors

Ben is a Certified SRI Counselor (CSRIC), an MBA, and an advocate for organizations and individuals looking to align their investments with their values. He draws from his experience working with asset managers, financial advisors, and industry insiders to help make sustainable investing accessible and achievable for even the most novice of investors.

In addition to his work with Till Investors, he is the Managing Director for the financial communications firm Purcell Communications, where he manages content for some of the largest financial institutions in the country. He is also an adjunct professor at Hood College, where he teaches courses on sustainable investing and social entrepreneurship.

He has published academic research on corporate social responsibility while also practicing what he preaches in his numerous Director-level corporate operational roles throughout his career. Drawing on his Project Management Professional (PMP) background, he is a pragmatist, and an ideal partner for Kyle's enthusiasm and vision. Ben constructs the practical pathways that make Till Investors a truly useful partner for sustainable investors.

Index

Avoiding strategy, 46–49

BlackRock iShares MSCI USA ESG
 Select ETF, 60, 61, 63, 64,
 107–108
 fact sheet, 60
 impact reports, 71
 performance commentaries, 68
 results, 65–66
 trail, 61
 U.S. Proxy Vote Guidelines, 63
 vote reports, 70

Calvert Equity Fund, 100–101
 fact sheet, 60
 Global Proxy Vote Guidelines, 63
 impact reports, 71
 performance commentaries, 68–69
 results, 67
 trail, 61–62
 vote reports, 70–71
Calvert equity fund, 60–64
Corporate social responsibility, 11

Diversity hiring, 2
Divesting/negative screening, 46–49
Domini funds, 104–105

Engagement, 53
Environmental, Social, and
 Governance (ESG), 12
ESG exchange-traded index fund
 (ETF), 59
ESG integration, 49, 50
Exchange-traded funds (ETFs), 38

Fact sheet, 60–62, 65–68
Fidelity, 111–112
Financial advisor (FA), 86–88
Forum for Sustainable and
 Responsible Investment, 5
Fossilfreefunds, 47
Fund manager profiles, 97–98

Goldman Sachs U.S. Equity ESG
 Fund, 72–73
 fact sheet, 60
 Global Proxy Voting Policy, 63–64
 impact reports, 71–72
 performance commentaries, 69
 results, 67–68
 trail, 62
 vote reports, 71
Green Century Funds, 106
Greenwashing
 greenwashing detective, 58–59
 scale of, 58
 shades, 57–58

Heavy greenwashing, 58
Heavy hitters, 8

Impact investing, 7
Impact reports, 71, 93
IMPAX, 102–103
Individual Retirement Account (IRA),
 37, 39
Influencing strategies, 51–54, 92
Institutional investors, 8
Intel, 30–31
Invesco, 113

Light greenwashing, 58

Materiality, 15–16
Morgan Stanley Capital International
 (MSCI), 60
MSCI ESG rating, Tesla, 19–21

Non-U.S. funds, 43

Parnassus, 98–99
PIMCO, 113
Principals of Responsible Investment,
 7
Proxy voting, 51–54
Putnam investments, 113

Racial diversity, 17
Retirement plan, 39–42
Rewarding, 49–51
Risk management, 26

Saturna Capital/Amana Mutual
    Funds, 106
Sin stocks, 6, 47
Small-cap funds, 43
Smart financial decisions, 12
Socially responsible mutual funds,
    6, 7
Stakeholder capitalism, 12
Standard greenwashing, 58
Sustainability, 12
    as foundation for long-term
        success, 29–31
    Intel, 30–31
    Toyota, 29–30
    what makes valuable,
        25–27
Sustainability Accounting Standards
    Board (SASB), 15
Sustainable company,
    11–22
Sustainable development goals
    (SDGs), 13, 14, 17
Sustainable funds, 31–33
    divesting/negative screening,
        46–49
    examples, 78–83
    fund profiles, 76
    influencing, 51–54
    issues, 75
    online search tool, 76–77
    options, 76
    rewarding, 49–51
    screens, 78

Sustainable investing, 5–9
    cost, 23–24, 31–33
    engagement with organizations,
        94, 95
    financial advisor (FA), 86–87
        finding right advisor, 87
        sustainability conversation with,
            88
    heavy hitters, 8
    ladder of impact, 35–44
        for beginners, 36–39
        retirement plan, 39–42
        sustainable portfolio building,
            42–44
    limitations, 6–7
    origins, 6–8
    right fund, finding, 45–55
    risk management, 27–28
        for-profit colleges, 27
        Juul e-Cigarettes case, 27–28
    sustainable funds
        divesting/negative screening,
            46–49
        influencing, 51–54
        rewarding, 49–51
    theory, 26
    U.S. Investors' Awareness, 6
Sustainalytics, 20, 21

Tesla, 18–21
Thematic funds, 43, 114–115
TIAA/Nuveen, 113–114
Toyota, 29–30
Triple bottom line, 12

Vanguard, 109–110

Workplace retirement plan, 40, 93–94

OTHER TITLES IN THE ENVIRONMENTAL AND SOCIAL SUSTAINABILITY FOR BUSINESS ADVANTAGE COLLECTION

Robert Sroufe, Duquesne University, Editor

- *Confronting the Storm* by David Ross
- *Sustainability for Retail* by Vilma Barr and Ken Nisch
- *People, Planet, Profit* by Kit Oung
- *Bringing Sustainability to the Ground Level* by Susan J. Gilbertz and Damon M. Hall
- *Handbook of Sustainable Development* by Radha R. Sharma
- *Community Engagement and Investment* by Alan S. Gutterman
- *Sustainability Standards and Instruments* by Alan S. Gutterman
- *Strategic Planning for Sustainability* by Alan S. Gutterman
- *Sustainability Reporting and Communications* by Alan S. Gutterman
- *Sustainability Leader in a Green Business Era* by Amr E. Sukkar
- *Managing Sustainability* by John Friedman
- *Human Resource Management for Organizational Sustainability* by Radha R. Sharma
- *Climate Change Management* by Huong Ha
- *Social Development Through Benevolent Business* by Kalyan Sankar Mandal
- *Developing Sustainable Supply Chains to Drive Value, Volume I* by Robert P. Sroufe and Steven A. Melnyk

Concise and Applied Business Books

The Collection listed above is one of 30 business subject collections that Business Expert Press has grown to make BEP a premiere publisher of print and digital books. Our concise and applied books are for…

- Professionals and Practitioners
- Faculty who adopt our books for courses
- Librarians who know that BEP's Digital Libraries are a unique way to offer students ebooks to download, not restricted with any digital rights management
- Executive Training Course Leaders
- Business Seminar Organizers

Business Expert Press books are for anyone who needs to dig deeper on business ideas, goals, and solutions to everyday problems. Whether one print book, one ebook, or buying a digital library of 110 ebooks, we remain the affordable and smart way to be business smart. For more information, please visit www.businessexpertpress.com, or contact sales@businessexpertpress.com.

www.ingramcontent.com/pod-product-compliance
Lightning Source LLC
Chambersburg PA
CBHW061330220326
41599CB00026B/5109